U0823134

孔子

CONFUCIUS

《孔子》摄制组　　著
闫东　主编

新世界出版社
NEW WORLD PRESS

First Edition 2018

Written by Documentary *Confucius* Project Team
Compiled by Yan Dong
Book Design by He Yuting

Copyright by New World Press, Beijing, China

All rights reserved. No part of this book may be reproduced in any form or by any means without permission in writing from the publisher.

ISBN 978-7-5104-6443-0

Published by
NEW WORLD PRESS
24 Baiwanzhuang Street, Beijing 100037, China

Distributed by
NEW WORLD PRESS
24 Baiwanzhuang Street, Beijing 100037, China
Tel: 86-10-68995968
Fax: 86-10-68998705
Website: www.nwp.com.cn
E-mail: nwpcd@sina.com

Printed in the People's Republic of China

目 录
CONTENTS

序一：在中英合拍纪录片《孔子》全球上线新闻发布会上的致辞 / i
Preface I: Address at the Global Press Conference for the Co-produced Documentary *Confucius* / i

序二：孔子就在我们身边 / xi
Preface II: The Confucius Who Is Just Around Us / xi

孔子其人 CONFUCIUS / 001

传说 THE LEGEND / 010

哲学 THE PHILOSOPHY / 030

至圣先师 THE GREAT SAGE & MASTER / 074

传承 A LIVING GOD / 088

当今 THE MODERN WORLD / 114

附录一：摄制组名单 / 144
Appendix I: Crew List / 145

附录二：主创人员简介 / 158
Appendix II: Main Crew Members / 159

附录三：中外专家点评纪录片《孔子》 / 172
Appendix III: Experts' Comments on *Confucius* / 173

附录四：学者评论 / 186
Appendix IV: Scholars' Comments / 187

附录五：孔子"和而不同"的思想指导我创作纪录片《孔子》 / 200
Appendix V: Application of the Confucian Concept of 'Harmony in Diversity' in the Production of *Confucius* / 201

后记 / 205
Afterword / 205

2015 年 10 月 22 日，在英国伦敦兰卡斯特宫纪录片《孔子》国际版上线新闻发布会上，中央电视台副总编辑李挺现场发言

Li Ting, Deputy Editor-in-Chief of China Central Television (CCTV), takes the floor at the Global Press Conference for the Documentary *Confucius* (international version). The conference was held in Lancaster Palace, London, on Oct. 22, 2015.

序一：在中英合拍纪录片《孔子》全球上线新闻发布会上的致辞

Preface I: Address at the Global Press Conference for the Co-produced Documentary *Confucius*

时值中国国家主席习近平访英期间，由中央电视台、中国国际电视总公司、英国雄狮公司和山东大众报业集团联合出品的展示中国古代思想家、教育家、儒家学派创始人孔子生平及其后世影响的大型纪录片《孔子》即将正式上线，与全世界观众见面。

孔子作为中华文明最具象征性的文化符号，已经成为一个世界性的热议话题。因此，作为国家媒体的中央电视台，全力打造一部多方位、立体呈现孔子生平及其丰厚的思想遗产的纪录片，是我们义不容辞的历史使命和文化担当。

孔子是中国文化的象征性人物，对中国思想文化的发展有极其深远的影响，也是世界上知名度最高的中国人。然而，孔子究竟是谁？他的一生有怎样的故事？这些故事怎样促使他创立了不朽的伦理道德哲学？孔子思想的核心是什么？他的思想为什么能成为治国之道、民族之根基且影响至今，这是一个怎样的过程？

自 2013 年 9 月起，中英创作团队历时两年的时间，克服重重困难，前所未有地深入到与孔子相关的人、地点、仪式中去，既包括了历史遗存，也容纳了当今发生的事件，展开了一系列紧张有序的采访和拍摄。摄制组在中国山东、北京、新疆、广东、湖南、湖北等地进行

The documentary *Confucius*, which was co-produced by CCTV, the China International Television Corporation (CITVC), Lion Television of the UK, and the Shandong Dazhong Newspaper Group, went online for a global audience during Xi Jinping's visit to the UK in 2015. The documentary presents the life and influence of Confucius, the ideologist, educator, and founder of Confucianism.

As a cultural icon of Chinese civilization, Confucius has been a hot topic of discussion across the world for centuries. CCTV, as a state-owned media outlet, took on the historical mission and cultural responsibility to make a multi-directional, stereoscopic documentary that presents the life and ideological heritage of Confucius.

As a symbolic figure of Chinese culture, Confucius has had a profound influence on China's ideological and cultural development. He is also the best-known Chinese in the world, though little about his life is known in the West. Who is Confucius? What is the story of his life? How did he found this ethical and moral philosophy? What is the core of Confucian ideology? How did his philosophy become the root of a nation?

For a period of two years beginning in September 2013, the Sino-UK creative team delved into the people, places and rituals related to Confucius, including historical relics and current events, and conducted a series of interviews and video recordings. The documentary was shot in Beijing and a number of provinces and regions, including Shandong, Xinjiang, Guangdong, Hunan, Hubei, etc. Through focus on the reunion scenes of ordinary Chinese people

了大量拍摄，特别是通过中国普通百姓回家过年等内容，把镜头对准了中国老百姓团圆的场景，纪实展现了儒家文化传统在现实生活中的意义。清明节期间，摄制组在山东曲阜忠实记录了 2015 年孔子家祭的全部过程。情景再现部分的拍摄，则对孔子的一生进行了详细解读。

纪录片《孔子》以精妙绝伦的场景、引人入胜的画面，完成了对孔子的历史与今天的呈现与穿越。这将是一次对孔子与儒家思想的终极的探索与发现，让全球观众了解到，当今孔子与儒家思想依然影响着中国与世界。

纪录片《孔子》的推出，旨在增强中华文化的国际理解，深化中西文化的交流融合。它将带领全球观众一起探寻孔子的生平与时代，以国际的视角，揭开孔子思想的奥妙。我们都想读懂中国，通过孔子，我们终于能实现了。

孔子创立的儒家学说以及在此基础上发展起来的儒家思想，对中华文明产生了深刻影响，是中国传统文化的重要组成部分。儒家思想同中华民族形成和发展过程中所产生的其他思想文化一道，记载了中华民族自古以来在建设家园的奋斗中开展的精神活动、进行的理性思维、创造的文化成果，反映了中华民族的精神追求，是中华民族生生不息、发展壮大的重要滋养。中华文明，不仅对中国发展产生了深刻影响，而且对人类文明进步

during holidays such as the Spring Festival, the documentary reveals in a tale-telling way the influence of traditional Confucian culture on real life. During Tomb-Sweeping Day in 2015, the crew of the documentary recorded the entire process of the Confucius Family Sacrifice in Qufu, Shandong Province.

While giving a detailed account of the life of Confucius, the documentary shuttles back and forth between Confucian time and China today through exquisite scenes and fascinating pictures so that the global audience may understand that Confucius and his ideology still have a great impact on China and the world.

The documentary was launched for the purpose of strengthening global understanding of Chinese culture and deepening the interchange and integration of Chinese and Western cultures. It will lead the global audience to explore the life and times of Confucius, and it will uncover the mysteries of Confucian thought from an international perspective. For those of us who want to understand China as it is, Confucius is certainly the key.

Confucian doctrine and the ideologies developed from it have had a profound influence on Chinese civilization and have become important components of traditional Chinese culture. Confucianism, together with other thoughts and cultures that emerged during the formation and development of the Chinese nation, chronicles the spiritual activities, rational thinking and cultural achievements of the Chinese people in the process of building their homeland. It reflects the nation's spiritual pursuit and nourishes its incessant growth

做出了重大贡献。

1582年，当利玛窦受意大利大主教委派，从遥远的西方文明国度意大利来到当时的明帝国，试图用天主教义来同化中国的时候，他在很多年里一无所成。1594年，他在一位中国儒生瞿太素的点拨下，脱下了曾经以为可以博取某种身份的僧袍，穿上儒服，戴上儒冠，摇身一变成为受人尊敬的“泰西硕儒”之后，他或许才真正理解了孔子之于这个古老而庞大的帝国的影响力之大。

正如他在《中国传教史》中所说：中国最伟大的哲学家是孔子。他所说的和他的生活态度，绝不逊于我们古代的哲学家；许多西方哲学家无法与他相提并论。故此，他所说的或所写的，没有一个中国人不奉为金科玉律；直到现在，所有的帝王都尊敬孔子，并感激他留下的遗产。

同一年，利玛窦出版了《四书》的拉丁文译本，这是儒家经典最早被译成西方文字。由于利玛窦在沟通中西文化方面做出的巨大贡献，他曾被雅称为“基督教的孔夫子”。

利玛窦和与之同期的传教士们，并没有在中国取得传教事业上的实质性的进展，却使得孔子这位中国古代先哲的著作得以远渡重洋，先在巴黎问世，随后被传向

and expansion. Chinese civilization has profoundly influenced its development and made a great contribution to the civilization of all human beings.

In 1582, Matteo Ricci, a Jesuit priest sent by the archbishop of Italy, came all the way from that civilized Western country to the Ming Empire of China. He spent years trying to assimilate China with Catholic doctrines, but ended up accomplishing nothing. Initially, Ricci dressed in the robe of a Buddhist monk, but in 1594, at the suggestion of the Chinese scholar Qu Taisu, he took on the silk gown of a Confucian mandarin. Perhaps not until he became a much respected Western scholar in China did he truly comprehend the magnitude of Confucian influence on this huge, ancient empire.

As Ricci said in *Chinese Missionary History*, "China's greatest philosopher is Confucius. Confucian teachings and ways of life are not inferior to those of our ancient philosophers, and many Western philosophers cannot even be compared to him. Therefore, what he said and wrote are considered golden laws and precious rules by all the Chinese people; all emperors honored Confucius and were grateful for his legacy."

The same year, Ricci published the Latin version of The Four Books (*The Great Learning, The Doctrine of the Mean, The Analects of Confucius* and *Mencius*), which composed the first translated Confucian classics in Western countries. Ricci was known as the Christian Confucius, due to his great contribution to the communication between Chinese and Western culture.

了更广阔的西方世界。

孔子思想影响广及海外，从启蒙运动的中国趣味到东亚文化圈，一直到现在的孔子学院，儒家作为世界重要的思想资源，孔子亦被认为是中国人对人类文明的伟大贡献。

纪录片《孔子》以开放性的当代视野，创新性的电视影像风格，讲述鲜活的故事，解读深邃的思想，站在历史与今天、中国与世界的高度，去发现孔子由凡而圣的生命历程及儒家文化的当代价值。在此，我们热切地期望，汇聚各方面精英力量创作出的纪录片《孔子》，能够为中外观众奉献一部值得长久记忆的经典作品。

李挺

中央电视台副总编辑

Instead of making any substantial progress in their missionary work in China, Ricci and his fellow missionaries took the works of Confucius across the sea, first to Paris and then further to the wider Western world.

The spread of Confucian influence overseas in modern history has passed through three major stages: The China interest during the Age of Enlightenment; East Asian cultural sphere; and Confucian institutes today. Because of the importance of Confucianism as a global ideology, Confucius is also considered a great Chinese contributor to human civilization.

Confucius tells fun and colorful stories and interprets profound ideologies in innovative audio-video form from an open, contemporary perspective. From the multidimensional vantage points of the past, present, China, and the world, the documentary explores the journey of Confucius from an ordinary man to a sage and unearths the values of Confucian culture that apply to the world today. We have every expectation that this documentary, a co-product of the elite from all circles, will be a memorable classic to global audiences for a long time to come.

Li Ting

Deputy Editor-in-Chief of CCTV

梁国典，山东大众报业集团社长

Liang Guodian, President of the Shandong Dazhong Newspaper Group

序二：
孔子就在我们身边

Preface II:
The Confucius Who Is Just Around Us

中英合拍纪录片《孔子》的诞生，让世界各地民众再次将目光聚焦中国，聚焦中国优秀传统文化，可谓意义重大。这也是继《孔子》动画片、电视剧、电影之后的又一文化力作，为孔子文化传播再添新亮点，也标志着中国优秀传统文化的数字化、全球化传播形态日益丰富。而作为参与其中的一分子，我也对能为孔子文化的现代化传播贡献一份心力而倍感荣幸和欣慰！

孔子作为中华文明和东方文明极具象征性的文化符号，已经成为全世界了解和认识中国的一个重要载体。早在 2007 年，我曾就职的中国孔子基金会就联合山东省委宣传部等单位，开始了以孔子为主题的文化产品的创意开发，先后打造了中国孔子网、新杏坛、动画片《孔子》、电视剧《孔子》等一批文化品牌项目，推动了孔子思想和儒家文化在海内外的传播。而对于《孔子》纪录片，我们也早在 2010 年就开始立项和筹备，并通过召开多次专家论证会，达成最终拍摄共识：就是要还原真实的孔子和孔子思想。不仅要有古人评孔子，还要有今人论孔子；不仅要有国人看孔子，还要有外国人看孔子；要以现代视野、世界眼光来看孔子、儒家文化在当代的价值，在

The release of *Confucius*, a Sino-UK co-produced documentary, is quite a phenomenon as it draws renewed worldwide attention to China and the elite of its traditional culture. The documentary is a new form of Confucius-related cultural masterpiece that comes on the heels of other Confucius-related art forms, such as cartoons, TV dramas and movies. It marks a new highpoint in the way Confucian culture is being disseminated, and it symbolizes the increase of diversified, digitalized and globalized dissemination of the elite of traditional Chinese culture. As a participant in this production process, I feel honored and pleased to have done my part to further the dissemination of Confucian culture through cutting-edge communication!

As a cultural icon of Chinese and even Eastern civilization, Confucius has become an important conduit for the world to know and understand China. As early as 2007, the China Confucius Foundation, where I was formerly employed, worked together with the Publicity Department of the Shandong Provincial Communist Party Committee and other authorities in developing Confucius-themed cultural products, culminating in the completion of a series of cultural brand programs including www.chinakongzi.org, a TV program on traditional Chinese culture called New Apricot Altar, an animated feature called *Confucius*, a TV drama of the same title, etc., that have played a part in promoting the dissemination of Confucian ideology and culture at home and abroad. Project proposal and preparation for the documentary *Confucius* began as early as 2010. After multiple meetings with experts, we reached a consensus about the focus of the documentary, which was to present the real Confucius and his

世界各文明中的地位。

2013年中央电视台加入了《孔子》纪录片项目，将其立项并全力以赴推进国际、国内版纪录片制作。多方合作之下，终于完成了有关中国伟大思想家、教育家孔子这个“最熟悉的陌生人”的国际化影像呈现。在国际社会了解中国的诉求越来越强烈的背景下，这部影片无疑是向世界讲好中国故事的一次有益尝试。对于当今的中国人，我们认同孔子是至圣先师，他所创立的儒家学说和在此基础上发展起来的儒家思想，已经成为中华民族的精神基因，融入了华人血脉。而他具体是怎样的一种存在？纪录片《孔子》给了我们一个梳理的机会，通过影片发现原来圣人不只是被高高地供起来的，其实他就在我们身边——与你我同行。

这么大的一个题材，能够通过90分钟时间展现出来，而且让观影的人觉得很有看头，这的确是比较难做的。影片选择了平实、朴素的手法，从最普通的个人出发来阐述孔子的大贤大智，将本应供在高处的概念拖回到现实生活中，让每一个人能亲切地贴近孔子。孔子其实跟当下的每个中国人都有关系，他的思想不仅在中国，在亚洲、

thought. We wanted to look at Confucius from different perspectives: Past, present, Chinese, and foreign. We wanted to see, with a modern and global vision, the value and status of Confucius and Confucian culture in the world today and among different civilizations.

In 2013, CCTV became a partner of the documentary project, initiated it, and fully-committed to producing the domestic and international versions of *Confucius*. Through multilateral cooperation, we finally completed the international version, thus giving new life to China's greatest thinker and educator, who has until recently been only the 'most familiar stranger' to the general audience. Given the backdrop of the international community's increased need to better understand China, this documentary is certainly a good and powerful attempt to properly convey the China story. Today, we Chinese recognize *Confucius* as the Great Sage and we venerate his school of thought, known as Confucianism, which has effectively become our spiritual DNA. However, what are the nuts and bolts of Confucius? The documentary gives us an opportunity to comb through the life and thinking of Confucius and learn that the Great Sage is not just up in a shrine for worship, but is actually around us and with us.

It was quite a challenge to present such a grand topic in an appealing way in just 90 minutes. So, in a plain and simple approach, the documentary drills down to real life transcendental concepts and illustrates the great virtues and wisdom of Confucius from the perspective of common people so everyone can feel close to Confucius. Confucius actually relates to every Chinese individual

在世界也都有其深远影响。看完影片，穿越了2500多年，你就会发现：孔子其实就在你身边！

90分钟国际版的完成刚让我们松口气，紧接着的六集长篇国内版又将开拍了。而今迈步从头越，以闫东为总导演的《孔子》摄制组全体成员们，继续加油吧！为自己为国家也为世界，为历史为今天也为未来，即使担子再重，我们必须全力完成这项历史使命，向大家交一份满意的答卷。

梁国典

影片总监制、山东大众报业集团社长、

前中国孔子基金会理事长

today, and his ideology profoundly influences China, Asia, and the entire world. After traveling with the documentary across over 2,500 years, you eventually realize how close to your life Confucius really is!

Having just celebrated the completion of the 90-minute international version, the crew of *Confucius,* led by Chief Director Yan Dong, are now ready to shoot a full-length, six-episode domestic version. Let's cheer them on as they undertake this new historic mission! However heavy the burden, we owe it to our country, the world, and to the past, present, and future. We must fully commit ourselves, and get this done right and well for every viewer.

Liang Guodian
Chief Producer of *Confucius*,
President of the Shandong Dazhong Newspaper Group and
former President of the China Confucius Foundation

究竟该如何讲述一个文明古国的故事，尤其是中国这样一个文化悠久、底蕴深厚的国度，回望历史或许只能有一种方式，那就是通过一个人的故事来认知这个国家，这个人就是孔子。

2,500 years ago, a man was born whose ideas would shape the lives of billions of people and the thinking of a nation. The country was China and his name was Kongzi, known in the West as Confucius.

孔子其人
CONFUCIUS

孔子画像

A portrait of Confucius

孔子诞生于2500多年前，那是一个礼坏乐崩、天下大乱的时代，而他穷其一生所开创的儒学思想，正是试图为那个王室衰微、诸侯争霸的时代重新建立秩序与和谐，并从此深深影响了中国乃至世界几十亿人的生活。

孔子的一生历尽挫折与磨难，他的思想和学说并没有被他的时代接受，然而在他辞世数百年之后，他的思想却逐渐成为中华文明的精髓所在。孔子的教育思想是中国传统的坚厚基石，已经沿用并发展了2000多年，而在社会伦理道德层面他提出的孝悌忠信和任人唯贤、为政以德的理论和主张，依旧深植于中国的政治和经济格局之中。孔子坚信“礼”是家国安定的关键，这种观念始终贯穿于中国社会的方方面面，上至国家典礼下到构成社会生活的核心单元家庭。

Born into an age of violence and war, Confucius was the creator of a political and moral philosophy that was designed to bring harmony to the chaos of his times.

His extraordinary story saw his ideas rejected in his own lifetime. However, they were adopted by China's emperors in the centuries after his death, and have survived China's rich and tumultuous history to influence countless lives, not just in Asia, but across the world. His teachings have been the foundation of Chinese education for nearly 2,000 years. His ideas of meritocracy, obedience, and moral leadership have profoundly shaped China's political and economic landscape. In addition, his belief in the power of ritual and etiquette to unite the nation still governs everything from ceremonies of state to the most important unit of Chinese life – the family.

悉尼大学王安国教授
PROF. JEFFREY RIEGEL, University of Sydney

悉尼大学王安国教授：

若想了解中国就必须理解孔子，以及他留下的思想和文化遗产。

孔子是中国历史上最伟大的思想家、教育家和政治家，然而他那些以身垂范的生平事迹，却在辞世近400年后才被后代史学家记录下来。也就在那个时代，历经数百年的动荡与战争，中国进入了一段相对和平与迅速繁荣的时期，许多延续至今的传统观念与文化习俗逐渐形成。这个经济与文化蓬勃发展的时代就是汉朝，在同一时期，除罗马外世界上再无一个国家可以与之相提并论。

JEFFREY RIEGEL:

To understand China, one must understand Confucius and his legacy.

The story of Confucius was first documented during the Han Dynasty, 400 years after his death. Following centuries of civil war, this was an era of peace and prosperity, of great innovation and scholarship, in which many of the customs and traditions that define China to this day were born.

司马迁是西汉时期的著名思想家和史学家，就在此时撰写出了中国第一部纪传体通史《史记》。《史记》中评述了不同朝代的君王和有着重要影响的人物，记载了他们的言行事迹以及家族世袭的谱系，《史记》中的《孔子世家》一章就是第一部关于孔子的传记。

西汉史学家司马迁（再现拍摄）
SIMA QIAN, a historian during the Western Han Dynasty (reproduction photography)

西汉史学家司马迁：天下君王至于贤人众矣，当时则荣没则已焉，孔子布衣传十余世，学者宗之。

At the heart of the court, the Grand Historian Sima Qian devoted his life to writing the first full history of China: The *Shiji* (*Records of the Grand Historian*). Contained within it is a narrative of the events, rulers, and families who made the most important contribution to the Chinese Empire, including the first known biography of Confucius.

SIMA QIAN: The world has known innumerable princes and worthies who enjoyed fame and honor in their day, but were forgotten after death. However, Confucius, a commoner, has been revered by scholars for over 10 generations.

《史记·孔子世家》不但记载了孔子的生平事迹和他的言论思想，也包含了司马迁对于孔子的评论和赞誉。时至今日，这段文字仍然是当代学者研究孔子最重要的史料依据。

耶鲁大学金安平教授
PROF. ANNPING CHIN, Yale University

耶鲁大学金安平教授：

颜回入见孔子曰，回诗云：匪兕匪虎率彼旷野，吾道非耶吾何为于此。司马迁所著的《孔子世家》之所以如此重要，是因为它是历史上首次尝试，真正的第一次将孔子逝世 300 年后出现的多个故事编纂在一起，通过一个连续的长篇传记还原孔子的一生。我认为司马迁对孔子人性化的一面非常关注，这么一个伟人不仅能够生存下来，还传承了重要的思想，教导我们如何做人，教导我们成为道德高尚的人。当然，孔子全然不知自己的言论最终会对中国人产生如此重要的影响。

A mixture of fact, oral history, and Sima Qian's imagination, this biography is still one of the main sources for the story of Confucius, and it documents the struggles he endured to get his ideas heard.

ANNPING CHIN:

Yan Hui came in and Confucius asked: '*The Book of Songs* says, "I am neither rhinoceros nor tiger, yet I made it to the wilderness." Is our way wrong? Is that why we have come to this?' The biography of Confucius by Sima Qian is so important because it's the very first attempt to draw together the many stories that had emerged in the 300 years since Confucius died. I think Sima Qian was acutely aware of this very human side of Confucius and of how such a man was able to survive and pass on something very important about being human. Of course, Confucius had no idea that whatever he said would eventually be so important to the Chinese.

传说
THE LEGEND

司马迁：孔子生鲁，昌平乡陬邑。生而首上圩顶，故因名曰丘云，字仲尼姓孔氏。

孔子的父亲曾是鲁国有名的武士，在与正室妻子生育了9个女儿之后，通过纳妾生下了儿子孟皮，却不幸患有足疾。这让他更加急切地盼望拥有一个身心健全的儿子作为家族的继承人，于是他又迎娶了当地一位17岁的少女。

SIMA QIAN: Confucius was born in the state of Lu in a village called Zouyi. He was born with a lump on his forehead that looked like a hillock, so he was given the personal name Qiu and the courtesy name Zhongni. His family name was Kong.

The father of Confucius, a retired military officer, had already fathered nine daughters with his first wife and a clubfooted son with his concubine. Desperate for a healthy male heir, he courted the 17-year-old daughter of a local family.

孔子 75 代后裔孔祥林
KONG XIANGLIN, descendant of Confucius

孔子 75 代后裔孔祥林：

孔子的父亲大概在 60 多岁的时候向颜家求婚，颜家就跟三个女儿商量，你们谁愿意嫁给他。老大老二都不吭声，谁愿意嫁给一个老头？但是小女儿说：父亲说谁嫁给他就谁嫁给他。所以第三个女儿颜徵在，就嫁给了孔子的父亲。

盼子心切的孔子父母于是去往当地有着“圣山”之称的尼山祈祷，渴望能够生下一个健康的儿子。

KONG XIANGLIN:

Thus, the father of Confucius, at age 60, proposed marriage to the Yan family. Mr. Yan asked his three daughters which one wanted to marry him. The two elder daughters said nothing. After all, who wants to marry an old man? The youngest daughter said her father should decide and therefore she, named Yan Zhengzai, married the father of Confucius.

Desperate to conceive, the parents of Confucius went to Mount Ni, a local sacred mountain, to pray for a son.

耶鲁大学金安平教授：

司马迁写道：孔子的父母在野外幽会，即“野合”后生下孔子。然而儒学家对此说法感到非常不满，但我认为这意味着孔子父亲60岁左右娶了当时十几岁的孔子母亲，在当时一个年老的男人和年轻女子的结合是不合礼制的，也就是说孔子从出生就不是一个平常人，他在成长过程中也必须解决很多难题。

《圣迹图》是中国最古老的连环画之一，这部作品就是根据司马迁所著的《孔子世家》绘制而成的。在山东曲阜的孔子档案馆，现在还珍藏着一版《圣迹图》的绘画本。《圣迹图》的刻绘始于15世纪，这一套版本描绘了孔子一生的传奇故事，其中最有名的就是关于孔子诞生的传说。

ANNPING CHIN:

Sima Qian said the parents of Confucius had a tryst in the wild. In Chinese this is *yehe*, and Confucian scholars are very uncomfortable with that idea. However, I think what this means is the father was about 60 when he had this relationship with the mother, who was in her teens, perhaps considered very inappropriate. So, it's also about 'Hey, Confucius was just very human from the beginning, with many problems to sort out as he grew up.'

Sima Qian's biography became the subject of one of China's oldest picture-book stories, called the *Traces of the Sage*, an edition of which has been carefully preserved in the *Confucius Archives* in his home province of Shandong. Dating from the 15th century, it also included many other legends that had surfaced regarding Confucius after his death, in particular the most famous version of his birth story.

北京外国语大学田辰山博士
Dr. TIAN CHENSHAN, Beijing Foreign Studies University

北京外国语大学田辰山博士：

这个非常生动，这个情景一看你自己就能进到这个情景当中去了。

《圣迹图》中的这幅场景描绘的是孔子的母亲在怀孕之时，曾经梦到了一种神秘的生物麒麟。这是一种集龙头、鹿身、蛇鳞于一身的象征着祥瑞之兆的神兽。在中国古代的神话传说中，每逢麒麟出现就表明会有大事发生，而孔子母亲的梦境正是预示着孔子诞生的超凡入圣。

《圣迹图》孔母梦麒麟

The mother of Confucius dreamed about Qilin in *Traces of the Sage*

DR. TIAN:

This version tells the story vividly; bringing the audience into the story.

This scene illustrates the visit to the mother of Confucius of a mythical creature called a *qilin*. Made from different animals – the head of a dragon, scales of a snake, and body of a deer, in Chinese mythology, the *qilin* traditionally heralded the arrival of a great event, but it also tells us something significant about Confucian humanity.

北京外国语大学田辰山博士：

在中国传统中，人们（看到麒麟）会想到鹿躯干的主要部分，是鹿反映了这种生物温和的特性，鹿不会伤害其他动物甚至不会踩踏到昆虫。我觉得这也是为什么麒麟在《圣迹图》中如此重要，就是为了告诉人们为什么孔子如此不同，他并不是凡夫俗子中的一员。

孔子 3 岁时父亲便去世了。从此之后，孔子与母亲就一直过着极其清贫的日子，《圣迹图》中也描画了孔子早年的这一段生活。作为士族阶层的一员，年轻的孔子曾担任过一些低微的官职，包括叫作“乘田”的畜牧管理员等职务。

《圣迹图》孔子早年生活

The early life of Confucius in the *Traces of the Sage*

DR. TIAN:

In Chinese tradition, people think of a deer, mainly the body of a deer, as reflecting a mild disposition and mild nature. Deer never harm other animals, never ever step on an insect. I believe this is why *qilin* was so significant in this story; to give people an idea of why Confucius is a very distinguished figure, not one of the ordinary people.

Raised in severe poverty after his father died when Confucius was only three years old, the *Traces of the Sage* tells the story of Confucius in his youth. As a member of the *shi* (scholar) class, the young Confucius took on a series of jobs, including managing the State's herds of oxen and sheep.

耶鲁大学金安平教授：

“士”可以翻译为许多意思，我个人倾向于把“士”理解为“绅士”，比平民百姓高一个阶层。而“士”与平民的区别就在于“士”能够接受教育。

于是，在孔子 30 多岁的时候，他决定创办私学，传授弟子，而他作为哲人的身份也由此开始。尽管最初的时候私学规模很小，但终其一生受教于孔子的学生超过了 3000 人。

ANNPING CHIN:

'*Shi*' – There are many ways to translate that character. '*Shi*' – I prefer the idea of the common gentleman. A common gentleman is just one level above a commoner. What makes him sort of distinct from a commoner is that a common gentleman is allowed to have an education.

As a result, after getting married in his 20s, Confucius decided to open a school from which his reputation as a philosopher would be born and that eventually (we are told) attracted over 3,000 students.

加州大学伯克利分校戴梅可教授
PROF. MICHAEL NYLAN, UC Berkeley

加州大学伯克利分校戴梅可教授:

这并不同于我们理解的办学,并不进行单纯的学术训练。如同希腊的早期哲人，孔子办学是为了帮助弟子在仕途上平步青云。因此，他的弟子，包括一些有权势的人、一些贵族阶层以及立志成为贤明统治者的人。

在孔子去世之后，孔子早年的教诲被他的弟子和再传弟子整理编撰成中国最经典的书籍之一《论语》。这本书是保存了孔子一生最重要的学说和思想的言行录。最初，《论语》是由孔子的弟子们将其言行思想刻写在竹简上的。年代最古老的

MICHAEL NYLAN:

It's not schooling in our sense: It's not academic training. As with the early ancient Greek philosophers, it's schooling in a way of life by powerful people, people with access to power, people with some leisure, and people who wish to rule wisely and well.

Over time, the teachings of Confucius would form the basis of one of China's most sacred texts: The *Analects*. A collection of the most important thoughts and sayings of Confucius, they have followed the development of Chinese civilization. Originally compiled by his disciples on fragile bamboo slips, the oldest fragments of the text

《论语》竹简残片，是在公元前55年的墓葬中被发现的。在孔子去世之后的数百年间，早已涌现出了多个流传于世的《论语》版本。公元2世纪，经过融合为一而最终确定的《论语》版本被雕刻在了石碑上。《论语》石碑就立在汉朝时候的中央官学太学之中，供学者们研究学习。而这个统一版本的《论语》也成了汉朝的专用教科书。

作为记录孔子的言行思想的重要典籍，2000多年以来，《论语》一直是中国大小课堂上被传诵的教材。

学而时习之不亦乐乎，有朋自远方来不亦乐乎，人不知而不愠，不亦君子乎。有子曰：其为人也孝悌。

子曰：三人行必有我师焉，择其善者而从之，其不善者而改之。

have been discovered in tombs dating from 55 BC and reveal circulation of different versions of the book in the centuries after his death. In the 2nd century, one definitive version was then 'fixed' by being carved onto stone. Erected in the Imperial Academy for scholars to study and learn, this version became one of the foundational texts of the Chinese Empire.

And this same text has been taught in schoolrooms across China for over 2,000 years.

CONFUCIUS said: When I walk along with two others, they may serve me as my teachers. I will select their good qualities and follow them, their bad qualities and avoid them. (*Analects* 7.21)

CONFUCIUS said: Is it not delightful to have friends coming from distant quarters? Is he not a man of complete virtue who feels no discomposure though men may take no note of him? (*Analects* 1.1)

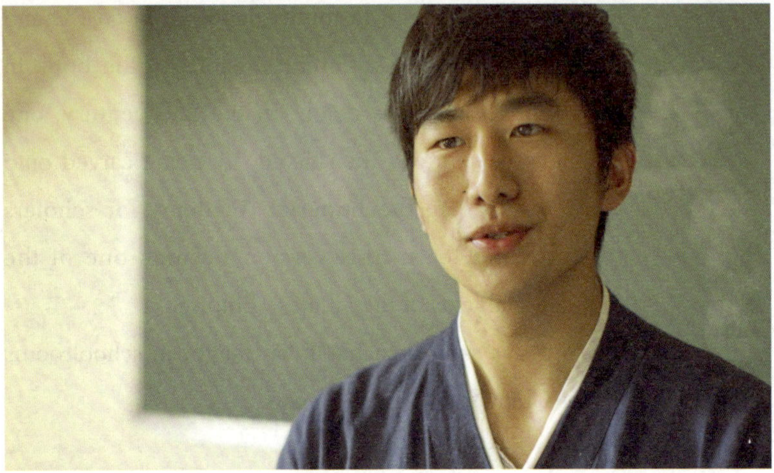

四海孔子书院吕云鹏老师
LV YUNPENG, teacher at the Sihai Confucius Academy

四海孔子书院吕云鹏老师：

《论语》作为儒家最重要的一部经典，当中记述的都是孔子和他弟子言行的汇集。在当初，孔夫子是怎么样教育他的子弟的，乃至于他的弟子门人一些对话的记录。

即使到了现在，《论语》也仍然是研究孔子哲学思想的主要依据。而其中所包含的道德准则，也早已成为中国传统文化的基石。

TEACHER LV YUNPENG:

The *Analects* is the most important book of the Confucian classics. It's a collection of the words and acts of Confucius and his disciples, and it records how Confucius enlightened his disciples and the conversations they had together.

The *Analects* is now the primary source of Confucian philosophy and contains the moral code that has become the cornerstone of Chinese traditional culture.

子曰：学而时习之不亦乐乎，乐悦同，学之为言效也，人性皆善而觉有先后。

四海孔子书院吕云鹏老师：

《论语》作为中国人的“圣经”，可以说是每一位中国人都应该读诵的一部经典。这里面都是关于古人讲的修身齐家治国平天下的道理。所以正如古人所言：半部《论语》可以治天下。

CONFUCIUS said: Learning is imitating. All men are born 'good.'

TEACHER LV YUNPENG:

The *Analects* is like the Chinese bible. It's a classic that every Chinese person must read. Its principles are self cultivation, family regulation, national order, and world harmony. There is a saying: 'With half of its knowledge, you can rule the world.'

哲学

THE PHILOSOPHY

孔子诞生于公元前551年，那是一个天下大乱、战火四起的时代。当时中国已经分为数个大小不一的诸侯国，那些春秋霸主们都试图以血腥的战争来扩大自己的疆域。

加州大学伯克利分校戴梅可教授：

孔子在其生活的年代，目睹的都是接连不断的战争，或是一国侵略另一国，或是国家统治者被行刺，或是国家迅速被消灭。

在孔子生活的时代，大约并存着12个经常互相征战的诸侯国。在黄河流域广袤平原的中心，散落着5个古老的小国，周围环绕着的则是一群实力很强的大国。

Born in 551 BC, Confucius lived in an age of political chaos and war. At this time, China was divided into numerous states, each locked in a desperate and bloody battle for domination of the country.

MICHAEL NYLAN:

Confucius was born in an era when all he saw around him was continual warfare. States fought each other, assassinated rulers, and extinguished kingdoms as quickly as they could.

At the time of Confucius, there were about 12 states fighting for their existence. A central core of around five smaller states was surrounded by a group of much larger and more powerful neighbours.

悉尼大学王安国教授：

孔子所在的国家即是其中一个小国，当时齐国统治者想要吞并鲁国。

孔子急切地想要寻找到能够解决迫在眉睫的战争局势的方法。他追溯历史，尤其想借鉴周朝初期的治国方略。那时的西周被称为“天下共主”，是距离孔子出生600年以前，周朝统治者在黄河流域建立的一个强盛王朝。

悉尼大学王安国教授：

包括孔子在内的许多人认为，周朝是一个黄金时期，那时统治者善施仁德，勤政爱民。

周朝与孔子所处的战乱时代不同。他认为周朝之所以和平稳定，很大程度上，是由于被国人尊奉的规范制度将周朝社会凝聚了起来，孔子将这种规范制度称为“礼”。

悉尼大学王安国教授：

礼从根本上说就是仪式礼仪，从更广泛的意义上，也指风俗和社会惯例。比如，如何问候老朋友，如何向师长和父母表达敬意等。孔子指出了这些风俗和社会惯例非常重要，

JEFFREY RIEGEL:

Confucius lived in one of the small states, known as Lu, which bordered the great state of Qi. There was no question that the rulers of Qi were intent on swallowing-up Lu.

Desperate to find a solution to the violence of his age, Confucius looked to the past. In particular, Confucius looked to the era of the early Zhou kings, who had ruled large parts of China 600 years before.

JEFFREY RIEGEL:

Many people, including Confucius, looked back to the Zhou as a golden age, as a time when rulers governed their people with virtue, kindness, and compassion.

Unlike the political disorder of his own time, Confucius believed the Zhou period was peaceful and stable, thanks in large part to the ancient rites, customs, and etiquette that bound Zhou society: A concept Confucius called 'li.'

JEFFREY RIEGEL:

'*Li*,' at its core, is ceremony and ritual. It also refers to what we think of more generally as custom and social practice: What I say when I greet an old friend; What I say when I express reverence for a teacher or parent. Confucius

像胶水一样凝聚整个社会。

孔子：道之以政齐之以刑，民免而无耻，道之以德齐之以礼，有耻且格。

为了更广泛地考察和学习周朝的礼乐文化，公元前518年，也就是孔子33岁的时候，他获得了君王鲁昭公的资助，离开鲁国开始了游学之路。鲁昭公派了一驾有着两匹马的车辆和两个僮仆协助孔子，经过长途跋涉，他们到达了当时周朝的东都洛邑（现在的洛阳）。

孔子75代后裔孔祥林：

为什么要到洛阳去呢？因为洛阳是当时的周朝的首都，因为国家的利益的那些规定，还有那些文献主要都在那儿保存着。孔子在洛阳的时候，还非常有幸见到了老子，因为老子是当时的柱下史，相当于现在的国家档案馆和国家图书馆的馆长，孔子也就能够更好地熟悉周代的这些文献，还有它的礼仪的规定。

pointed out how very important those customs and practices were as the glue of society to keep us together.

CONFUCIUS said: If the people are led by penal laws, they will try to avoid the punishment, but have no sense of shame. If they are led by virtue and the rules of propriety, they will have a sense of shame and will become good. (*Analects*, 2.3)

To learn about the ancient rites and customs first-hand, in 518 BC, at age 33, Confucius was granted permission to leave the state. Given a carriage and two horses, he travelled a great distance to the ancient capital of the Zhou kings in modern-day Luoyang.

KONG XIANGLIN:

Why Luoyang? Because Luoyang was the capital of the Zhou Dynasty and all documents of ancient rules and etiquette were kept there. Confucius was very lucky because he had met Laozi in Luoyang, whose title was equivalent to today's curator of the National Archives and National Library. Therefore, he was able to better understand these classic documents from the Zhou Dynasty, along with Zhou etiquette and rituals.

孔子要学习的首要礼仪便是祭祀时的礼仪，尤其是祭祀先人的礼仪，祭祀活动是周人“敬天法祖”、宣扬天人合一的关键。

加州大学伯克利分校戴梅可教授：

当我们谈到许多礼仪的时候，我们是指血祭，以血或者酒作为祭品，祭祀我们天上的祖先与神灵。我们的祖先在去世之后升入天堂变成神仙。但是祭祀时并不仅仅献祭酒肉，每次祭祀必须带着崇高的敬意。每次祭祀，祭祀者怀念着并想象着祖先的样子，仿佛祖先又再次回到人世。这种祭祀确实非常虔诚，你的肉体尚存在于世间，但是精神得到升华。

耶鲁大学金安平教授：

一个人祭祀自己祖先的感觉和祭祀天上神灵的感觉截然不同。

周王祭祀使用的方鼎
The Square Tripot used in ancient sacrifices of the Zhou kings

The rituals that Confucius went to study in Luoyang were first and foremost the sacred rites, in particular the ancestral rites that were essential in keeping the human world in harmony with the cosmos.

MICHAEL NYLAN:

When we talk about many of the rites, what we're talking about are blood sacrifices, offerings of blood and wine, and they're offered to the ancestors and the gods in Heaven. The ancestors lived in Heaven and became gods in the afterlife. But, one doesn't just set out meat and wine. In each offering, one must bring a particular attitude of reverence. The reimagining of the ancestors in a sense brings them back to life with each offering. There's really a kind of religiosity in it. You're still grounded in the human world, but there's elevation.

ANNPING CHIN:

One has to very clearly distinguish that kind of religious experience from a religious experience that involves a creator with a force that's outside the human world.

这一尊距今已 3000 多年的方鼎，是专供周王祭祀时使用的礼器，现藏于北京的中国国家博物馆。这些珍贵的文物，包括形制庞大的祭祀方鼎、令人瞠目的青铜编钟以及精巧的酒器，均证明了中国青铜文明的博大精深。但对于孔子来说，它们还传达了一个清晰的信息，这些在那个时代被用来打造兵器的精良技术，同样可以用来制作祈求和平与安宁的礼器。

夏威夷大学安乐哲教授
PROF. ROGER AMES, University of Hawaii

夏威夷大学安乐哲教授：

在那个时期，人类文化开始出现审美，提升人性、摒弃兽性，开始追求高贵、复杂、文雅和迷人的事物。孔子身处一个混乱的年代，试图重建周礼。因为周礼随着空前爆发的战争而逐渐衰微。

The vessels used in these ancient sacrifices of the Zhou kings are now held in the National Museum of China in Beijing. From enormous sacrificial bowls and stunning sets of bronze bells to intricately cast drinking vessels, these artifacts testify to the sophistication of Chinese Bronze Age culture. Yet, for Confucius, they also conveyed a clear message, as the the same skills that were used to create weapons of war in his own age could once again be used to create objects of harmony and peace.

ROGER AMES:

What happened during this period was the lifting of human beings out of our animality, making us into something elegant and enchanted. Confucius, at the beginning of a very troubled period, tried to re-establish this, the '*li*' that had faltered as China had become increasingly involved in war.

如果说祭祀祖先的目的在于“慎终追远”，达到“和”的境界，那么，依孔子所言，社会和谐的理想状态，就能够通过施行并强化数百种日常生活的礼仪得以实现。这些小的礼节，从拱手问候到长幼、师生、夫妻之间的尊重关系，依然存在于中国人的生活中。

清华大学贝淡宁教授
PROF. DANIEL BELL, Tsinghua University

清华大学贝淡宁教授：

礼的目的在于，让人通过守礼产生集体归属感与被关怀感，而由此产生的许多礼仪，包括集体聚餐和家庭聚餐时必须长者先动筷子，包括与家人和师长饮酒时，晚辈和学生必须像这样避开长辈喝酒。虽然这些礼仪等级森严，但这些礼仪的最终目的在于使守礼者感受到关爱，这是其他方式所无法替代的。

If the ancestral rites aimed for 'cosmic harmony,' then Confucius believed social harmony could be achieved by reinforcement of the hundreds of smaller rituals that still govern Chinese life – from handshakes and greetings to the relationships between young and old, teacher and student, or husband and wife.

DANIEL BELL:

The aim of '*li*' is to generate a sense of community and caring among the participants of that ritual. Thus, you have rituals like group eating. If you're sitting among family, the elder person usually eats first. When drinking rituals include the family and the teacher, the student is supposed to drink without facing the teacher. These are hierarchical rituals, but again the ultimate purpose of these rituals is to develop a sense of caring among the participants that would not otherwise be the case.

耶鲁大学金安平教授：

孔子的智慧在于他意识到，他所做的是传递一些业已存在的事物，存在于家庭和社会的日常实践中，这些礼仪和规范并不是随意的，已经被人们用时间检验过了。

如今孔子生活过的地方，曾经的鲁国都城曲阜已经成为中国最具历史价值的地方之一。其中著名的景点就是三孔：孔庙、孔府、孔林。最负盛名的首推孔庙，这座祭祀孔子的庙宇，在中国是建筑规模仅次于故宫的古文化建筑群。与孔庙相邻的孔府，象征着主人的尊贵家世，是孔子的嫡子嫡孙们居住的地方。曲阜的边界，便是孔林，是孔子及其后裔的家族墓地。依据司马迁所著的《孔子世家》中的记载，孔子在曲阜达到了其政治成就的最高峰。孔子 50 岁时，因为政绩卓著而晋升为鲁国大司寇、摄相事主管司法，于是他试图通过推行“礼”来改变国家的命运。

ANNPING CHIN:

The genius of Confucius lies in the realization that what he was doing was transmitting something that was already in everyday practice within a family, within a community. Thus, these ritual practices were not arbitrary, but had been tested over time by others.

Today, the ancient town where Confucius grew up is called Qufu. Now one of China's most historic cities, it is home to what we call the 'three Confucian sites.' The first is the Temple of Confucius, the largest cultural complex in China after the Forbidden City in Beijing. Next door is the Kong Family Mansion, where his later descendants were honored and lived in splendour. On the edge of town is the Cemetery of Confucius, where Confucius himself is buried, surrounded by generations of his family. In Sima Qian's biography, Qufu was also the setting for Confucius' greatest political success. By the age of 50, Confucius had entered local government and had been promoted to the role of *sikou*, the Minister of Justice, in which he implemented his ideas of '*li*' and transformed the fortunes of his state.

曲阜孔庙

The Temple of Confucius, Qufu City

孔府

The Kong Family Mansion

孔林

The Cemetery of Confucius

孔子 75 代后裔孔祥林：

孔子做了这个行政长官以后，他就制定了一整套的礼仪规范。他根据人的身体的强弱来分配工作、根据人的年龄大小来分配食物。而且在市场上，这个卖牛羊的，他再也不敢一早把牛羊灌得饱饱的去卖了，他们要按重量称，早晨起来多喝点水就能多卖钱，他坑人。到了孔子以后，就没有这些了，所以鲁国治理得非常好。

耶鲁大学金安平教授：

我认为司马迁想强调孔子不愿通过刑罚管教人们，而是通过礼仪来教化民众。只有通过礼仪，人们才有羞耻之心，认识到自己的错误，从而想要改正自己的错误。

在过去的几十年中，儒家在《论语》中阐释的礼，在中国重新焕发出生命力。北东野村距离曲阜仅有一小时的车程，在这里，我们能够看到孔子所倡导的文明精神，儒家礼学已经融入了村民们的日常生活之中。

KONG XIANGLIN:

Once in this post, Confucius established a set of rules and guidelines governing the etiquette and formalities of the state. He assigned work to people according to their strength and age. In the marketplace, cattle sellers no longer overfed their cows and sheep or made them drink water in the morning to increase their weight and cheat people out of money. Under Confucius, there was no such thing: He really governed the State of Lu very well.

ANNPING CHIN:

I think Sima Qian really wanted to emphasize that Confucius educated through ritual practice, not penal laws. It was through ritual practice that people developed a sense of self-reform, realized their own wrongdoings, and wanted to correct those wrongdoings.

Over the past few decades, Confucian concepts of *li* in the *Analects* have seen a huge revival across China. As part of this revival, in Beidongye Village, just an hour's drive from Qufu, the morality of the *Analects* has been woven into daily village life.

山东省泗水县北东野村村长庞德海
PANG DEHAI, Director, Beidongye Village, Sishui County, Shandong

山东省泗水县北东野村村长庞德海：

养不教父母过，它的意思就是当父母的生养孩子，你不教育就是父母的过错；言必行行必果，说话要守信用，行动要有结果。

在过去的两年中，村委会为村民开办了儒学课堂。从每天早上广播《弟子规》开始。

山东省泗水县北东野村村长庞德海：

俺村里呢，我每天早晨都在 7 点半的时候，给村民放《弟子规》。每天早晨放一次，咱通过放《弟子规》来提高村民的思想觉悟，来建设咱的和谐村庄。

PANG DEHAI:

'Yang bu jiao, fu zhi guo' means to be reared without teaching is the fault of the parents. 'Yan bi xin, xing bi guo' means you should be true in word and resolute in deed.

For the past two years, the Beidongye Village committee has introduced Confucian lectures to the villagers, which begin with a daily broadcast of the *Standards for Being a Good Student and Child.*

PANG DEHAI:

Every morning, at 7:30, I start to play *Standards for Being a Good Student and Child* to the entire village. We play it hoping to elevate the moral awareness of the masses and build a harmonious village.

弟子规，父母呼应勿缓，父母命行勿懒，冬则温夏则凊，晨则省昏则定，出必告反必面，居有常业无变，事虽小勿擅为，苟擅为子道亏，物虽小勿私藏。

弟子规，圣人训，首孝悌，次谨信，泛爱众。

山东省泗水县北东野村村长庞德海：

通过这些年的学习，咱村确实发生了不少变化。原来不太孝顺老人的，变得孝顺了；妯娌之间不团结的，变得团结了；邻里之间也更加和谐了。俺村里有一个媳妇比较恶，曾经打过她婆婆，学习《弟子规》，她到书院参加学习了三次，她确实是发生了不少变化。她也感觉到自己做得不对了，为什么感觉不对？打老人本身属于不光彩的事。通过学习，我发现像俺村这种例子还很多很多的，这是其中的一个。我这个村领导也好干了。

对孔子来说，“礼”的教化似乎可以带领鲁国走向繁荣和强盛。然而，与他同时代的政治家们，开始采用阴谋策略来对付他。鲁国在孔子的治理下正迅速地崛起，这让与之相邻的齐国感觉到威胁并开始设计破坏鲁国的振兴计划。这一阴谋举措，从此彻底改变了孔子的未来命运。

The standards for being a good student and child are taught by ancient sages. First, treat your parents with filial respect and practice loving brotherhood. Second, learn to be discreet and trustworthy.

PANG DEHAI:

As a result of this educational program, there have been changes. Those who were not filial to the elderly are filial now. Arguments among sister-in-law arguments are less frequent. Relationships among neighbors are more harmonious. There is a wicked daughter-in-law in our village who hit her mother-in-law. After learning the *Standards for Being a Good Student and Child*, and attending three lectures, she has changed enormously: She realized that hitting the elderly is disgraceful. This is just one of many examples in my village. As the headman of the village, my work is now easier.

During the life of Confucius, reintegration of the ancient rites and customs had transformed the prosperity of his state, but the politics of his age soon conspired against him. *Traces of the Sage* tells the story that, threatened by the state's rise under the guidance of Confucius, Qi state hatched a plan that would have profound consequences on his life.

《圣迹图》中的故事是这样讲述的：公元前497年，齐国送了80名舞姬及120匹宝马给鲁国，国君鲁定公接受了女乐文马，于是，开始迷恋声色不理朝政，鲁国的礼仪也随之荒废。

《圣迹图》女乐文马
Female musicians, dancers, and colorful horses in *Traces of the Sage*

北京外国语大学田辰山博士：

女乐文马，这个马的数量跟这个女士的数量都不是记载的那个数量。这幅画非常重要，很关键，是孔子一生的转折点。他有几次试图劝谏鲁定公，你应该回归朝野治理你的国家，但最终还是没能奏效。这个国家对他来说，已经没有希望不值得留恋。于是，他离开去往别处，另外找寻能够实现理想的地方。

In 497 BC, the State of Qi sent 120 of its finest horses and 80 of its most beautiful dancers to Duke Ding of Lu. The Duke was so entranced that he neglected court rituals and sacred rites, causing the *li* of the state to collapse in just three days.

DR. TIAN:

This picture is known as Handsome Horses and Beautiful Women. The number of horses and female musicians are not the same as that recorded in history. This picture is significant, a key turning point in the life of Confucius. He tried in vain to persuade Duke Ding of Lu to take care of state affairs, leaving no hope for him to continue in his role. Thus, Confucius had to try another way, in another place, to realize his will.

失望之极的孔子终于离开鲁国，开始了一场逐梦之旅。他与追随着他的几位最衷心的弟子周游在正经受着战火洗礼的国家中，期盼着会有一位明君能够接纳并推行他的政治理想。

北京外国语大学田辰山博士：

在周游列国的过程中，孔子试图践行他的主张，劝说一些国君接受他的思想。他的理念主要就是如何将社会管理好，师生一同通力合作，他们一起赶路、相互帮扶，把他们的想法凝结成完整的思想体系。

这是孔子一生中最为后人津津乐道的时期之一。在此后的 14 年里，孔子一行游走于中原地区的 8 个国家之中。在每个国家所停留的时间从几周到几年不等。这是一段极其漫长而艰险的旅程，由于诸侯国之间持续不断的战火，孔子和他的弟子们常常居无定所，而人身安全更是无从保障，常常遭遇绑架迷路的危险，多次濒临死亡。

Despondent, Confucius decided to leave. Joined by a group of his most loyal disciples, he travelled across China's war-torn states in an attempt to persuade other rulers to adopt his ideas.

DR. TIAN:

On this trip, one thing he tried was to practice his ideas, to try to persuade all the kings to accept his philosophy on how to govern a good society. They work together, travel together, help each other, and contribute their own ideas into a pool of rich philosophy.

This is one of the most famous periods in the life of Confucius. During the next 14 years, Confucius travelled back and forth between eight of the smaller states in China's central plains, spending years in some and weeks in others. It was a long, arduous journey. Caught in the crossfire of states at war and without shelter or security, they had been kidnapped, lost, and, on many occasions, came close to death.

孔子 75 代后裔孔祥林：

他在这个路上遭到很多灾难。在宋国的时候，司马桓魋曾经要杀他们；在这个匡，让人家围起来以后不让他走；在陈蔡那个地方，七天七夜都吃不上饭，把弟子们饿得都爬不起来了。他在周游列国的时候很艰难困苦。

他们所经历的这些艰难困境，也促使孔子将自己的儒学理论进一步凝练。这段时期，孔子提出了他对后世影响最为深远的思想之一——君子。

孔子：这次我们周游列国，我最深的体会是：君子喻于义，小人喻于利。

清华大学贝淡宁教授：

“君子”通常翻译为道德高尚之人或绅士，但更好的译法是将其译为“楷模”。因为根据儒家理论，不论男女都应该努力成为一名“君子”，而立志成为君子者，则应有仁爱之心，不仅关怀家人还追求正义与道德，不把自己的个人利益放在首位，这种追求将持续其终生永无止境。

KONG XIANGLIN:

Confucius encountered many hardships along the way. In the state of Song, Sima Huantui wanted to kill him. In the state of Chen, people surrounded him in the city of Kuang and wouldn't let him leave. Stranded between the states of Chen and Cai, they ran out of food for a week: His disciples didn't have energy to move.

The challenges they faced forced Confucius to reflect upon and refine his philosophy. It was during this time that he developed one of his most profound ideas: The concept of the *junzi* (the morally noble or superior man).

CONFUCIUS: The mind of the superior man, the *junzi*, is conversant with righteousness. The mind of the inferior man, the *xiaoren*, is conversant with gain. (*Analects*, 4.16).

DANIEL BELL:

A *junzi*, normally translated as noble man, or gentleman, is better translated as an 'exemplary person' because, whether a man or woman, we should all strive to be *junzi* according to Confucian tradition. Somebody who strives to be a *junzi* should try to extend love and care beyond the family, care about justice and morality, and not place their own self-interest first and foremost: It's a never-ending, lifelong struggle.

相对于那些同时代的以武力安邦的统治者，孔子坚信一个真正的君子要以德治国，要把百姓的利益看得和自己的一样重要。

四川大学谢幼田教授
PROF. XIE YOUTIAN, Sichuan University

四川大学谢幼田教授：

在政治学里，始终一个最根本的问题就是约束权力的问题。皇帝有权力，所以儒家设计了一整套东西来约束皇帝，也就是后来儒家的政治哲学——爱民，所谓的爱民如子。

Unlike the rulers of his own age, who ruled by the sword, Confucius believed a true *junzi* ruled with virtue, putting his people's well-being alongside his own.

PROF. XIE YOUTIAN:

The principal issue in politics is to restrain power. Kings have power, so Confucianism consists of an entire set of thoughts to restrain kings. It is the Confucian political philosophy that a king should love his people as he loves his son.

不仅如此，更为重要的是孔子还给“君子”一词赋予了全新的内涵。在孔子之前，“君子”指“血统高贵的人”，而从孔子开始，“君子”则被解释为“品德高尚之人”。

悉尼大学王安国教授：

这确实有着革命性的意义。他鼓励人们去追求权力之外的东西，表面之下的东西，也就是我们所说的内在美、美德等品质，这是他在周游期间所取得的成就之一。

孔子的弟子们就是孔子对“君子”一词重新定义之后的最好例证，他们来自社会的各个阶层，没有一个出身高贵，但是却都具有成为“具有高贵人格的人”的潜质。

耶鲁大学金安平教授：

孔子的弟子来自社会的各个阶层，子贡过去是一个商人；子路有着武士的气质；他最喜欢的徒弟颜回来自平民阶层，家境非常贫寒；而仲弓的出身，在我看来其实是十分可疑的。我非常喜欢孔子对于仲弓的描述，他说一头耕地的老黄牛也可能会生出一头皮毛光滑、牛角漂亮的小牛。我想这都表明孔子并不以一个人的出身来评判这个人。

However, Confucius also gave the term a radical new meaning. Before Confucius, a *junzi* meant someone of noble blood; afterwards, it meant someone of noble character.

JEFFREY RIEGEL:

This is something quite revolutionary in that Confucius is inviting people to look beyond the trappings of power and physical attractiveness to what we may call inner beauty, virtue, ethics, and the like. This is one of the things I think he realized during his exile.

The disciples of Confucius are the best examples of his reinterpretation of the word *junzi*. Drawn from every section of society, none was of noble birth, yet all had the innate potential to be noble of character.

ANNPING CHIN:

Among his disciples, there were all types: Zigong was a merchant; Zilu was a warrior type; Yan Hui (one of his favorite disciples) was from a commoner's background, a very poor family; and the provenance of Zhonggong (another favorite) was very questionable. I love the description Confucius gave of Zhonggong: He said it's possible for a descendant of plough cattle to be born with perfectly formed

清华大学贝淡宁教授：

在当时，孔子非常在意对下一代的培养，力求使他们可以成为优秀的并且道德高尚的领导者，这种思想我们也可以称其为精英政治。整个政治系统的建立，应该以选择能力突出又道德高尚的领导者为目标，这是《论语》的中心思想，也是儒家传统的中心思想。

孔子的关于“礼”和“君子”的这些传统儒家思想，不仅适用于未来的领导者，也适用于中国人社会生活中最为重要的单位——家庭。每逢中国农历新年，成千上万人都会从全国各地回到自己的家乡，这堪称地球上最为壮观的人类迁徙活动。

2015 年农历腊月二十九的广州火车站
Guangzhou Railway Station on December 29, 2015 (lunar calendar)

horns. I think what all this tells us is that Confucius did not measure a person's worth by family background.

DANIEL BELL:

At the time, Confucius was very concerned with training future generations so they could be good and moral leaders. Thus, the idea of political meritocracy, that the political system should be designed to select rulers with superior ability and virtue, is central to the *Analects* and the entire Confucian tradition.

These ideals didn't just apply to potential rulers: *Li* and *junzi* found their origin in the most important unit in Chinese life – the family. During Chinese New Year, millions of workers from all over China return home in what is the largest mass migration of humans on the planet.

一年一度的春节大团聚，体现着孔子的儒家思想里最重要的内容，他管这种思想叫作“孝”，通常解释为“孝道”。“孝”字上面的偏旁代表“老”，下面的“子”代表年轻人。“孝”字从老从子，形象地揭示了年轻人应该尊重自己的长辈。“孝”在儒家思想中有着极为重要的地位，甚至还以此衍生出了《孝经》。

身体发肤，受之父母，不敢毁伤，孝之始也。

建筑工人张艳阳：

子曰：孝子之事亲也，居则致其敬（乐），养则致其乐，病则致其忧，丧则致其哀，祭则致其严，五者备也然后能事亲。

当下时代中国经济的腾飞式发展，也导致了许多外地务工人员常年与家人分居千里之外。对于很多打工者来说，春节或许是一年里仅有的一次归家团聚的机会。

At the heart of this celebration is another of the most important concepts of Confucius, what he called *xiào*, often translated as 'filial piety.' Consisting of the Chinese character for old above the character for young, filial piety illustrates the respect the young must pay to their elders and ancestors. Over time, filial piety became so important to Confucian thinking that it developed its own manual: The *Book of Filial Piety*.

CONFUCIUS said: The body, hair, and skin were all received from parents, and so one doesn't dare damage them. This is the beginning of filial piety. (*Book of Filial Piety*)

ZHANG YANYANG:

CONFUCIUS said: 'This is how a filial child serves his parents: During daily living, he exhibits respect; when providing for them, he exhibits happiness; during their illnesses, he exhibits worry; during mourning, he exhibits grief; when making offerings, he exhibits reverence. When he is prepared to do these five things, he is able to serve his parents.'

The reality of China's economic boom means that many families now live thousands of miles apart, and

建筑工人张艳阳
ZHANG YANYANG, Scaffolder

建筑工人张艳阳:

我现在回湖南衡阳老家，我也好几年没有回家了，都在外面。我老妈身体不好，我小孩一直都带在身边。我母亲这个思想，好像有点像小孩子那一种，怕孤单，所以要给点时间陪她。

乘客:

你比我幸运，我都 13 年没回家过春节了。

建筑工人张艳阳:

13 年不容易啊！ 13 年不容易，13 年好漫长的。

乘客:

挺快的，对我来说非常快，我工作都 13 年了。

张艳阳妻子:

我觉得很煎熬，我就算一年不回家看一次我老爸，我都觉得很煎熬，因为我太想他，因为他也在想我。

for many migrant workers, Chinese New Year is the only time in the year they can return home to see their parents.

ZHANG YANYANG:

I'm heading back to my hometown, Hengyang in Hunan Province. I haven't been back for quite a few years. My mother is not in good health, so I always bring my child with us. Older people are more like kids. They fear being alone. So, we should spend time with them.

PASSENGER:

You are luckier than me. I haven't been back for 13 years.

ZHANG YANYANG:

13 years! That's too hard for me. That's not easy. That's too long.

PASSENGER:

It's fast to me. I started my career 13 years ago.

ZHANG YANYANG's wife:

I would suffer even if I didn't go home for one year. I'd suffer if I couldn't see my dad since I miss him so much and he misses me the most.

依据司马迁在《史记·孔子世家》中的记载，可以了解，在孔子还很小的时候，他就懂得了孝的道理。孔子不玩其他小孩子所喜欢的那些玩具，而是把演习各种祭祀仪式作为童年的娱乐方式。随着孔子逐渐长大，他也慢慢体会到了关于家庭的一种价值观，那就是一个人对自己长辈的爱与尊敬可以延伸到整个社会，并由此提升整个社会的价值取向。

耶鲁大学金安平教授：

这应该是理所当然的事，年轻的人理应尊重年长的人，在村庄里年长的人应该优先享用食物。我认为孔子的天才之处在于，他为这些行动找到了一个道德基础。这个道德基础是什么呢？就是移情。他认为移情能力是区别人类和动物的要素，既然我们生而具有移情的能力，为什么不发展它呢？为什么不让它服务于家庭、服务于社会、服务于国家呢？

对于所有中国人而言，春节就意味着能够回到家乡与家人团聚。对于一个大家庭来说，是最为和美、最为欢乐的时候。在年夜饭之前，祭祖是中国人的传统习俗。在中国人的观念里，这种类似于宗教的信仰并不是信仰神明，而是信仰祖先、信仰家族的历史传承。

In Sima Qian's biography, we are told that filial piety came to Confucius naturally from an early age. Rather than playing with normal toys, Confucius spent his childhood staging ancestral rites for his father, who died when he was only three. As Confucius grew, he realized that the values he found in the family, exemplified by the love one had for one's parents and grandparents, could be extended outward for the benefit of society.

ANNPING CHIN:

I think his genius was he realized that there's a moral grounding to those practices: This moral grounding has to do with empathy. He thought of empathy as the one thing that distinguished humans from other animals. He thought if we are born with that sense, with that sort of stirring of empathy, why not expand it? Why not make it work for the family, the community, the state.

For all Chinese, the heart of the Spring Festival celebrations is the gathering of the family in the family home. But, before the dinner on Chinese New Year's Eve, it's customary to honor one's ancestors because religion in China isn't to a God, it's to one's shared past.

建筑工人张艳阳：

来，拜一下祖宗，保佑你们身体健康、年年会读书。

孔子认为这就是人的信仰所在，在家庭祭拜时通过这种仪式，人们学会成为一个君子、一个有道德的人。

建筑工人张艳阳：

我其实是一个孝顺儿子，我想，让我妈妈一个人在家其实就是不孝。年代不同，年轻人压力大，所以造成我这样的现象是很多的，确实很多。老年人像我妈妈我可以这样说，如果是我老妈她不是得那个病，我百分之百把她带出去了，我也不会让她一个人待在家里。最大的心愿我要把这个古老的房子解决掉，让我老妈住上洋房，现代式的洋房，让她享一享现代式的清福，这是普天之下做儿女的一份心。

ZHANG YANYANG:

Let's bow to the ancestors. Let's pray for you all to be healthy and do well at school every year.

In Confucian thought, Chinese religiosity lies in the family. It's through rituals like these that one learns to become a *junzi* – a moral person.

ZHANG YANYANG:

I am a filial child. However, when I think about my mother staying at home alone, I am actually not filial. Times have changed and young people now have much more pressure on them than before. I think a situation like mine is very common. If my mother didn't have dementia, I would 100% take her with me to the city. I wouldn't leave her at home. My biggest wish is to rebuild this old house and let my mother live in a modern, foreign-style house so she can enjoy herself. This is the wish of all sons and daughters in this world.

至圣先师

THE GREAT SAGE & MASTER

公元前 484 年，14 年之久的漫长而无奈的逐梦之旅终于宣告结束，孔子放弃了他济世安民的政治抱负返回家乡。由于没有任何一个诸侯国的君主接纳他的思想和主张，孔子决定将注意力转移到下一代君子的培养上。

耶鲁大学金安平教授：

那时他已经 68 岁了，曾经有人邀请他回来，回到家乡。据说，前来求教的年轻人挤破了他的大门，他们到底要从孔子那里学到什么呢？我觉得是治理的艺术。因为他的几个重要弟子都在政府里担任要职，比如说子贡就担任过政府官员，子路有很高的政治地位，还有仲弓，史籍记载他是地方长官。所以，这些年轻人可能认为，孔子可教给他们管理国家的方法、治理的艺术，甚至进入政府的门路。

In 484 BC, after 14 long years on the road, Confucius abandoned politics and finally returned home. Unable to convince any rulers to adopt his ideas, Confucius instead transferred his attention to training a new generation of *junzi*.

ANNPING CHIN:

By this time, Confucius was around 68 years old. His gate was just flooded with young men who wanted to learn from him. What did they want to learn? I think it had to do with the art of government because several of his chief disciples actually became very important people in government. Zigong served as a councilor, Zilu had a high political position, and Zhonggong was an administrator. Maybe these young men felt that Confucius could teach them something about statecraft, the art of government, and how to enter government.

孔子：博学于文约之以礼，亦可以弗畔矣夫。

为了培养下一代，孔子开创了从古代教化的原理中演化出来的课程，这套课程的核心就是六艺，一个君子培养独立人格所必须精通的六种技能。六艺包括礼、乐，它们都能为社会带来秩序与和谐。除此之外，孔子还设置了书（书法）、数（算数）、御（驾车）、射（射箭）这几项技艺的学习。最重要的是，据说在那个时期，孔子编纂了在中国历史上被儒家奉为典范之作的典籍，也就是现在所称的“儒经”。

孔子 75 代后裔孔祥林：

所以，他大概就想到把他的思想要传流下去，怎么办呢？就是整理古代的文献，把自己的思想都注入这个古代的文献当中去。所以孔子到了他的晚年这几年，他主要就是整理古代的文献；再一个就是教育他的弟子，当然也希望他的弟子能够把这个思想传承，还一个呢，宣传出去。

孔子开创的私学，也被后人描绘到了《圣迹图》之中。这幅著名的图画，生动地展现着至圣先师孔子与弟子们一起讨论并注解古代典籍的场景。

CONFUCIUS: By extensively studying all learning, and keeping oneself restrained by the rules of propriety, one may thus not err from what is right.

To train this new generation, Confucius developed a curriculum based on the ancient teachings of the past. At its heart were the Six Arts; those six skills a *junzi* needed to master to cultivate his character. They included *li* (the rites) and *yue* (music), both of which brought harmony to society. Confucius placed these alongside the essential skills of *shu* (calligraphy), *shù* (mathematics), *yu* (chariotteering), and *she* (archery). Most importantly, it was during this period that Confucius is said to have compiled and edited the ancient and most sacred books of Chinese history, which are now called the Six Classics.

KONG XIANGLIN:

Confucius thought he needed to pass his ideas on to future generations. By compiling the ancient literature and integrating his own ideas into them, Confucius hoped his thoughts would be inherited and spread by his students.

The Academy of Confucius is the subject of one of the most well-known paintings in the *Traces of the Sage*. It vividly depicts the Master and his disciples annotating and discussing the ancient literature.

《圣迹图》孔子注解古代典籍

Confucius annotating the ancient literature in *Traces of the Sage*

北京外国语大学田辰山博士：

大家可以看到这些人正在讨论古代典籍，热切地讨论，激烈地讨论。这里是孔子本人，8 个人围坐在他身边，老师和学生一起产生新的想法，年轻的一代完全沉浸在讨论中，参与到继承传统学术的活动中，这也正好映射了儒家在历史上发展的过程。

DR. TIAN:

In this painting, you see the people working on the classical texts, participating in warm discussion, sometimes heated discussion. Here, Confucius himself, with one, two, three, four, five, six, seven, eight people sitting around him, is the master with his disciples, together developing new ideas. The younger generation is entirely involved in the discussion on the continuity of tradition. This precisely reflects the idea and how Confucianism developed over history.

孔子删定“六经”的故事，在汉代成为最引人关注的话题。公元170年，这几部儒家经典被刻在了《熹平石经》上，这个权威的版本随后成为科举考试的基础教科书。科举是一种不论社会阶层和出身背景都可以参加的考试，用来选拔最优秀、最贤良的士子担任官吏。

悉尼大学王安国教授：

考试确保考生们学习了古代经典，并理解古代圣人的教化。如果他们理解了，那么可以认为他们对皇帝来说是统治内值得信赖的顾问或官员。

在接下来的十几个世纪中，后世学者的一些著作与注解文献也逐渐被列入了典籍之中，到了北宋时期，扩充成了“十三经”并得到了官方的认可。在北京的国子监，一共放置了189块石碑，石碑上的儒家经典共计63万字，花费了长达4年之久的时间才镌刻完成。

五年春王正月，辛亥朔日有食之，夏归粟于蔡。

苦其心志，劳其筋骨，饿其体肤，空乏其身。

The Six Classics (the *Book of Songs*, *Book of History*, *Book of Changes*, *Book of Rites*, *Book of Music*, and *Spring and Autumn Annals*) were canonized alongside the *Analects* during the Han Dynasty, in 170. Enshrined by the emperor in the Imperial Academy, these sacred books became the basis of China's famous Imperial Examination System, a rigorous set of exams designed to identify the most talented candidates for imperial government.

JEFFREY RIEGEL:

The examinations guaranteed that examination candidates had read the Classics and understood the teachings of the sages. If they understood those teachings, it was assumed they would be trusted as advisors to the emperor and trusted officials throughout his realm.

Over the following centuries, with books and commentaries added by scholars, the number of Classics grew to reach 13 by the period of the Northern Song Dynasty: These 13 Classics were all approved by the officials. At the Imperial Academy in Beijing, there are 189 stone steles containing 630,000 characters of the Classics that took over four years to carve.

MICHELLE: It's the fifth year of Duke Ding of the Lu State, the first month. The first day is 'Xinhai'

加州大学伯克利分校戴梅可教授：

我认为所有的早期文明，研究他们的历史不能仅着眼于过去。很重要的一点是，过去的历史教给后人如何为人处世，怎样激励人民，如何度过危机，怎样应对灾难，所有这些都在“儒经”中有所体现，还有大量的注解。

从隋朝到清末，科举制实行了 1300 多年，而考试一直以严苛著称。临场的考生们必须把大量的经典原文熟记于心，考试的答卷时间会持续 3 天，而晋阶之路共分 4 级，从最低级的童生试到最后在皇宫内举行的殿试，通过率仅有 1% 到 2%，因为只有少数的成功者才拥有晋身官场的可能，有些考生也会为了通过考试难关不择手段。

(traditional calendar, the 48th/60 day). There is a solar eclipse. In summer, Lu State sends millet to Cai State. (*Spring and Autumn Annals*)

OLDER MAN: When Heaven is about to confer a great office on any man, it first exercises his mind with suffering and his sinews and bones with toil.

MICHAEL NYLAN:

I think in all early civilizations, learning about one's many pasts, not a single past, is very important because past history provides precedent about what works, how you motivate people, what you do during crisis, and how you resolve dilemmas: All this is contained within the Confucius Classics and the various commentarial traditions.

The examinations themselves were famously rigorous. Candidates had to learn hundreds of thousands of passages from the Classic texts, with question and answer sessions lasting over three days. Conducted in four stages – from the lowest level country exams to the final imperial exams – the pass rate was only one or two percent. With such power and privilege awaiting the successful few, some candidates tried every method to succeed.

孔子 76 代后裔孔哲
KONG ZHE, a 76th generation descendant of Confucius

孔子 76 代后裔孔哲：

这些东西就是古代科举考试中常用的作弊的东西，它叫作夹带。它有两种质地，你可以看到上面那个是丝质的，底下这个是纸质的，它都比较适合用墨在上面进行书写。比如说，考生们会把它放在那边，像考篮里，像这个文具，考生们会把毛笔的中间弄空，把这东西搓成一个小卷放在里面，或者放在砚台底下，放在各种各样的夹层里，比如说衣服上、鞋子里。有时候，监考官会甚至要求考生脱掉衣服赤身裸体，因为有些考生他们有时候会把这些文字写在他们的肌肤上。因为一旦他们通过了这个考试，他们就会成为官员，他们就会获得相应的财富、获得相应的权力，就使得他们凌驾于普通人之上，所以这就相当于一道分水岭，在这边就是地狱，在那边就是天堂。

KONG ZHE:

Candidates used objects called '*jiadai*' to cheat during imperial examinations. There were two kinds of materials; one silk and the other paper, both perfect for writing on with ink. They hid them in exam baskets, hollowed-out writing brushes, under ink stones, or in the nooks of their clothing or shoes. Sometimes candidates would be required to strip and be checked naked because some of them might write on their skin. Once a candidate passed the imperial exams, he became a government official, superior to commoners, and was awarded fortune and privilege. This was a watershed moment, on one side Hell, on the other Heaven.

科举考试制度在后来广泛传播到了亚洲的其他地区，它影响的国家包括越南、朝鲜和日本等，不过科举考试在今天的中国最明显的传承也许就是高考。一年一度的大学入学考试，成千上万的学生为此拼命一搏，并非如古代一样是为了踏上仕途，而是为了让自己能够踏进全国最好的大学。出于对孔夫子的虔诚膜拜，许多学生都会按照惯例来到北京国子监，祈求至圣先师的保佑。

孔圣人，愿你能保佑我考到我心仪的学府。

愿我的一切努力都能得到回报。

孔夫子，希望可以做一个像你一样的人，把学习作为一生的乐趣，不只是为了考试。

The influence of the Imperial Examination System was so enormous that it spread across Asia to Vietnam, Korea, and Japan. Perhaps its clearest legacy in modern China is the national college entrance examination, in which students from all walks of life attempt to win places, not in government, but at the nation's best universities. As a mark of their debt to Confucius, one rite of passage for many students is a trip to the Imperial Academy in Beijing, where they ask for the blessings of China's greatest sage.

BOY:

Saint Confucius, please bless me to be admitted by my dream school.

GIRL A:

I hope all my efforts will be rewarded.

GIRL B:

Saint Confucius, I hope I can be like you and study as a life-long interest, not just for exams.

传承
A LIVING GOD

在过去的几十年间，成百上千座汉代陵墓在中国各地被发现，其中很多甚至可以追溯到公元 1 世纪，这些墓室内的汉画像石展现着汉代人对于世界的丰富想象，画面令人惊叹。墓室顶部的天界画满了神兽和祥鸟的形象，画壁两侧描绘的则是汉代马车和车夫所代表的俗世生活。如果说秦始皇在公元前 221 年实现了中国地理上的疆域大一统，那么汉朝在此后 400 年间的统治则是实现了中国文化上的大一统。因此，在这些古老的墓室中，人们可以看见象征着汉朝强盛的各种神话传说、风土人情和历史人物，这其中就包括已知最早的孔子画像《孔子见老子图》。

Over the past few decades, hundreds of Han Dynasty tombs have been discovered across China, many dating from around the 1st century, 500 years after the death of Confucius. Inside are stunning representations of the Han Dynasty's vision of the world: Heaven above, full of birds and beasts, with the human world of horses and charioteers below. If the first Emperor of the Qin Dynasty united the country geographically in 221 BC, then it was the following Han Dynasty that united it culturally over the next 400 years of its rule. Thus, within these tombs we see the establishment of the cultural heroes that underpinned China's emerging national identity, including the first-known portrait of Confucius.

汉画像石《孔子见老子图》
A Meeting of Confucius and Laozi, a stone relief in the Han Dynasty

山东石刻艺术博物馆研究员蒋英炬：

孔子的形象一般看成什么呢？他就是像一般官吏的形象，戴着前高后低的帽子叫“进贤冠”。有时候，手里执一个贽，就是贽鸟那个贽，手贽礼，这是一种古代的礼节。

汉画像石上的人物，通常会按照各自身份的不同而雕刻于不同的位置。士大夫位于底层，而神仙居于上层，每个人物的位置都和他们的尊卑程度有关。

山东石刻艺术博物馆研究员蒋英炬
DR. JIANG YINGJU, a researcher in the Shandong Stone Carving Art Museum

DR. JIANG:

Confucius often appears as an administrator with an official hat and gown. He sometimes has his hands clasped, which is ancient etiquette.

Figures on Han Dynasty tombstones were often carved in different tiers, with court officials at the bottom and gods at the top. Each figure's placement was relative to the esteem in which they were held.

山东石刻艺术博物馆研究员蒋英炬：

孔子的画像形象，一般在建筑物尤其在祠堂里，都画在屋的上部，墙壁的上部。为什么画在上部？一个就是对孔子的尊崇敬仰，敬仰嘛，仰就是往上看；另外一个是对儒家思想的一种敬仰和崇拜，这是他对孔子的，也是一种生前的尊重，死后也要崇敬这样的人物。

通过司马迁撰写的关于孔子的传记，我们可以知道孔子的生命历程里其实充满着挫折和磨难，在他的那个时代，没有一位在位的统治者愿意接受他创建性的思想。孔子去世之后，他的弟子与学生们坚持传播他的思想，直到汉代终于成为大一统王朝的正统思想。

孔子 75 代后裔孔祥林：

孔子他那个思想不是适用于那个时代的，所以，他的思想是适合于什么呢？是国家统一以后，能够使国家安定下来，使社会、使人民都能够和谐相处的这么一个思想。

在接续下来的十几个世纪中，孔子的思想对帝制中国发挥着至关重要的教化作用，每个县都要为孔子建立庙宇，把他的地位提升到了“天纵之圣”的高度。

DR. JIANG:

Confucius is usually painted on the top tier. One reason is to show reverence toward Confucius. 'Looking up' shows reverence. The other is to show respect and admiration toward Confucianism. This is to show respect to Confucius both in life and in the afterlife.

In Sima Qian's biography, we are told that Confucius died a frustrated man, having failed to convince a single ruler to take on his revolutionary ideas. After his death, his students and disciples insisted on spreading his thoughts. It was only in the Han Dynasty that his ideas emerged to become the dominant philosophy of a now united empire.

KONG XIANGLIN:

The politics of Confucius were not suitable for his own time: They were only suitable after the country had been united. Then, his ideas could stabilize the country and help create a harmonious society, a purpose to which his ideas were suitable.

Over successive centuries, the ideas of Confucius became so important to imperial China that every new prefecture erected a temple in his honor, elevating him to the status of a god.

加州大学伯克利分校戴梅可教授：

“神”这个词翻译过来就是神灵或者精神，简单说就是有重大影响的不可见力量。所以，可以有代表山川雨云的神，或者是那些对他们周遭有重大影响的、活着或者死去的存在，这就是为什么孔子是神。

始建于 1302 年的北京孔庙，在今天已经成为一个祭祀孔子的著名场所。孔庙坐落在国子监旁边，在过去的十几年里，孔哲一直供职于这里，负责北京孔庙的日常管理和维护事务。孔哲是孔子的第 76 代嫡系子孙。

孔子 76 代后裔孔哲：

我是出生在孔府里面的。从小在曲阜的孔庙里跑着、玩耍着长大。所以，这座孔庙对我而言，它的气味让我感到非常的熟悉，很像我家乡的感觉。

这里也是古代皇帝亲自祭祀孔子的地方，这一祭拜孔子的传统始于公元前 195 年的汉高祖时期，一直延续到 1911 年中国的最后一位皇帝宣布退位。

MICHAEL NYLAN:

'*Shen*' in Chinese, which we translate as god or spirit, means an unseen influence that has an enormous impact. Thus, you can have gods that represent mountains, rivers, rain, and clouds, or beings, living or dead, that exert an enormous impact on their surroundings. This is the sense in which Confucius is a god.

First established in 1302, the Temple of Confucius in Beijing is now the most well-known place devoted to the worship of Confucius. Located next to the Imperial Academy, for the past 10 years it has been under the care of Kong Zhe, a 76th generation descendant of Confucius himself.

KONG ZHE:

I was born in the Kong Family Mansion and grew up playing around in the Temple of Confucius in Qufu. Therefore, this temple feels very familiar to me, just like my hometown.

It was here where the emperor himself came to conduct sacrifices to Confucius, a tradition that started in 195 BC and lasted until the fall of the last emperor in 1911.

孔子 76 代后裔孔哲：

当皇帝亲自来的时候，他就要在紫禁城里起得非常非常非常早，半夜就要起来，然后沐浴更衣，做好一切的准备。然后，由他的车驾带领着到这个地方来祭祀。祭品的准备，首先要提到中国最传统的几样祭祀祭品，牛、猪、羊，我们叫“三牲”。在这个地方，皇帝要向孔子的神位上香；要把这个酒斟到这个爵里，就是古代的酒杯，同时还要读一些祝，这个祝就是祭文，上面写了，我们是如何如何敬仰孔子，大概就是这个意思吧！

这些祭奠礼的仪式，说明了“礼”在帝制时代的中国国家典礼上的重要地位，同时也显示了“孝”在古代中国的社会生活中的重要性。

KONG ZHE:

The emperor would get up very early in the Forbidden City. He would get up just after midnight, take a bath, and put on clean clothes. Then, he would take the imperial carriage here to offer sacrifice. Many offerings are prepared. The most traditional Chinese sacrifices include an ox, a pig, and a sheep. They are called the 'Three Sacrifices.' The emperor offers incense to the tablet of Confucius and pours wine into a '*jue*,' which is an ancient vessel, while reading commemorative texts about how much we revere Confucius.

These rituals reveal how China's emperors had restored the ancient rites of the Zhou kings to the heart of state life, but they also highlight the importance of filial piety to imperial China.

悉尼大学王安国教授：

“孝”的思想在帝制中国时期非常重要，因为随着儒家思想的发展，国家被看作一个庞大的家庭，就像“孝”能够连系家庭一样，它也能凝聚整个国家。

汉朝时期“孝”，在中国文化里最突出的体现，便是将整个孔氏家族提升到了朝廷显贵的地位。在孔子去世 500 年之后，经过浩繁的搜集整理，孔氏家庭的族谱第一次编定完成。孔子被尊为孔氏家族的第一位祖先，并且由孔子的嫡长子孙世袭继承“衍圣公”的爵位。

JEFFREY RIEGEL:

The idea of filial piety was important in imperial times because as Confucian ideology developed, the state was seen as the family on a large scale. Just as filial piety could bind together a family, so could it bind together an empire and ensure that subjects of that empire would revere the ruler. The ruler, in turn, would embrace and care for all of his subjects.

During the Han Dynasty, the best example of the importance of filial piety in imperial culture was the elevation of the family of Confucius, the Kongs, to Chinese nobility. 500 years after his death, the family tree of Confucius was painstakingly retraced and Confucius was appointed First Ancestor to a long line of Kong family members, with the principal male line eventually inheriting the title 'Duke of Kong.'

孔子 75 代后裔孔祥林：

因为中国的传统，是有恩就要报答。按照中国的传统，孔子对后人有恩德，后人就要报答孔子，就要给孔子的后代以优待。所以，从公元元年那一年，孔子的后代就被封作了一个侯爵——保成侯。到了唐代的时候，晋升了一个公爵，这个公爵一直延续到什么时候呢，一直延续到 1935 年，到 1935 年的时候，共和制度了，就不能保留公爵了，就改为了奉祀官。

如今，孔氏族谱已经记录了 2000 多年，孔氏家族也变得越来越庞大。目前，为了更好地编纂和修缮族谱，孔氏一族专门成立了自己的管理机构，这就是曲阜的孔氏族谱研究中心。所有的孔氏家族档案都完整地保存在这里，并由孔子的第 77 代嫡系子孙孔德铭保管着。

KONG XIANGLIN:

One Chinese tradition is that 'kindness should be repaid.' To repay the contribution Confucius had made, descendants of Confucius needed to be given privileges. Thus, in 1 AD, his descendants were honored with the title Marquis of Baocheng. During the Tang Dynasty, they were made Dukes. This lasted until 1935, when China became a Republic. At that point, the title of Duke was abolished and changed to an inheritable government post in charge of sacrificial ceremonies.

Within 2,000 years of genealogical records, the extended Kong family is now so big that it has its own headquarters, the Confucius Genealogy Research Center in Qufu. It's here where all Kong family records are kept under lock and key by a 77th generation descendant of Confucius, Kong Deming.

孔子 77 代后裔孔德铭
KONG DEMING, a 77th generation descendant of Confucius

孔子 77 代后裔孔德铭：

这一个房间是收录了我们所有孔子后裔世家谱续修期间保存的最原始的档案资料，对我们孔氏家族管理这一块，从政府这个行列也管理很严格，应该说是孔家人也享受一定的税收（优惠），或者是免一些兵役，另外就是，我们续修家谱也对我们孔子后裔，辨别孔子后裔真伪（有帮助）。

KONG DEMING:

This room contains all the records of the descendants of Confucius, including all family books and the original family tree. In terms of managing our family, it is very strict. Families of descendants have enjoyed certain benefits like tax reduction or exemption from military service. The compilation of the genealogy helps us verify the authenticity of real descendants.

2009年，孔德铭发布了最新续修的更为完整的孔氏族谱。这是近半个世纪以来，对于族谱的第一次续修。孔氏族谱共80卷，耗时12年完成，里面收录了200多万的孔氏后人。

孔子77代后裔孔德铭：

一开始作为孔子后裔，感觉做这个事情也是应该的。但是，随着家谱续修我们工作逐步地深入，我也是感觉到这个使命感和光荣感、自豪感也是越来越强，我感觉这个应该说是我这一生当中最大的一个收获。

孔子77代后裔孔德平

KONG DEPING, a 77th generation descendant of Confucius

In 2009, Kong Deming unveiled a new edition of the complete Kong family tree, which hadn't been updated for over half a century. Consisting of 80 volumes, it took 12 years to complete and contains over 2 million names, including women for the first time.

KONG DEMING:

When I began, I felt obliged to do this because I'm a descendant of the Kong family. However, later, with the process of the work, my feelings of pride and honor became increasingly stronger. I feel this has been the biggest achievement of my life.

孔子 77 代嫡孙女孔德懋
KONG DEMAO, a 77th generation descendant of Confucius

被誉为“天下第一大家”的孔氏家族，他们的族谱已经成为历史上最久远、最庞大的家族谱系，囊括了生活在世界各地的超过200万的嫡系子孙。

孔子76代后裔孔令珊
KONG LINGSHAN, a 76th generation descendant of Confucius

孔子76代后裔孔令珊：

因为从孔子文化来讲，我们姓孔的对孔子文化有很深的情怀，所以我们姓孔的后代感到自豪，有无比的信心和力量。

Often referred to in Chinese as 'the first family under Heaven,' the Kong family's genealogy is now the oldest and longest accredited family tree in history, with over two million descendants living all over the world.

KONG LINGSHAN:

As descendants of Confucius, people from the Kong family have a deep feeling toward Confucius. We're so proud of our surname. We have inimitable confidence and power.

孔子 77 代后裔孔凯蒂
KAITY TONG, a 77th generation descendant of Confucius

孔子 77 代后裔孔凯蒂：

我叫孔凯蒂，是孔子第 77 代后人。我的名字凯蒂（恺悌）取自《孝经》，是我爷爷给我起的，这个名字的意思是“王子一般的品质”，王子的品质。

KAITY TONG:

My name is Kaity Tong. I'm a 77th generation descendant of Confucius, and my name, Kaity, in fact, is derived from the Confucian *Classics of Filial Piety*. My grandfather named me. Actually, what my name means is to have princely qualities, the qualities of a prince.

孔子 79 代后裔孔垂旭
JAMES KONG, a 79th generation descendant of Confucius

孔子 79 代后裔孔垂旭：

大家好，谢谢你们邀请我来这里，我叫詹姆斯 · 孔，中文名是孔垂旭，我是第 79 代孙。

作为孔氏一脉的嫡系子孙，他们既沐浴着家族的光辉，同时也会背负着压力。孔氏家族的每一位成员，无论生活在世界的哪一个角落，都要以儒家的道德准则来要求和规范自己。

JAMES KONG:

Hello everyone, thank you for having me here today to speak to you. My name is James Kong, or in Chinese, Kong Chai Shu. I am a 79th generation descendant of Confucius. My grandfather is the head of the family, and most direct line, in China.

Being a Kong also brings its own pressures. For the prestige of their family name, every Kong is expected to uphold the values of Confucian morality wherever he or she lives.

孔子 77 代后裔孔凯蒂：

在我的成长过程中，我的母亲一直灌输给我们，你是孔家的一员，是孔子的后人，行为举止不能有偏差。在学校，你一定要比别人做得好，你要更强壮、更聪明，时刻记住为你的家族争光。整个孔氏家族和中国人都在你小小的肩膀上，那时我 5 岁。

孔子 79 代后裔孔垂旭：

作为孔子的第 79 代后人，我有一份额外的责任，我必须端正举止，为他人树立榜样，每一天我都在努力做正确的事，并希望能鼓励他人同我一样。

KAITY TONG:

When I was growing up, my mother pounded that into our heads. You are a member of the Confucius family. You're a descendant of Confucius, so don't misbehave. When you go to school, you have to be better, stronger, smarter, and remember that the honor of your family, the Confucian family, and all the Chinese people rests on your tiny little shoulders. I was five years old at the time.

JAMES KONG:

As a 79th generation descendant of Confucius, I have an extra level of responsibility in the manner in which I behave and the example I set for others. Every day, I work toward this good behavior in myself and hope it inspires other people to do the same.

当今
THE MODERN WORLD

儒家提倡传承古代传统文化和思想，为此招来其他学派数不胜数的抨击，这其中包括孔子同时代的论敌以及他去世之后若干个世纪里的否定者。而发生在20世纪的风起云涌的批判浪潮，则产生了最深远的影响。这种批判的浪潮，在20世纪六七十年代的“文革”中达到顶点。为了尽快让中国与当代世界接轨，孔子被归类为“四旧”的代表，即“旧思想、旧文化、旧风俗、旧习惯”。

Confucianism's emphasis on hierarchy, tradition, and ancient etiquette has made it the focus of numerous attacks from alternative schools of thought, both during the lifetime of Confucius and in the many centuries after his death. In the 20th century, imperial traditions were often blamed for China's poverty and lack of development. Given that Confucianism was the mainstream tradition, it became a principal target. By the late 1960s, Confucius was included in what was called the Four Olds: Old culture, old ideology, old customs, and old habits.

曲阜文保所办公室前主任高景鸿
GAO JINGHONG, Former Director of the Relic Protection Center in Qufu

曲阜文保所办公室前主任高景鸿：

红卫兵造反，这是把孔府大门的门匾扯下来以后。

这一时期因为孔子和中国封建帝制的紧密联系，与他相关的很多遗迹被相继毁掉。而在他的故乡曲阜——三孔的所在地，一些文物侥幸被当地政府以特殊的方式保护了下来。

GAO JINGHONG:

This is when the Red Guard was here. This is after the rebels took down the board on the gate of the Kong Family Mansion. They were propagandizing to the public in front of the gate.

At the height of this period, due to the strong association of Confucius with China's feudal imperial past, his legacy was dismantled. This occurred nowhere more so than in his hometown of Qufu, where the three Confucian sites had to be placed under state protection.

曲阜文保所办公室前主任高景鸿：

因为我们是国家工作人员，那个时候国务院就在孔府门口立了一个石碑，保护文物石碑，（孔府）是国家重点文物保护单位。我们就把像上头石拱这种国家一级文物都埋到地底下了，把这个遗物和字画都藏到天花板上面。因为这些文物是不可再生的，是国家的宝贝，当时像周总理说的那样，你把这个破坏了以后，你就不知道历史了。因为我是接受这样的思想，所以我那个时候，就没参加造反派。

在过去的40年中，随着中国的现代化大发展和经济的腾飞，人们开始以一种全新的自豪感，重新拥抱传统道德与传统文化。而在举国上下对于儒家思想的高度重视下，孔子也重新成为中华文明源远流长的象征。在国家媒体上，孔子的学说和思想以具有新时代特色的方式被重新解读。在全国各地的一些普通学校里，儒学也回到了教学课程的核心内容中。

GAO JINGHONG:

Because we were protecting the cultural relics on behalf of the state, the State Council put up a plaque saying 'Key cultural relics site under state protection' just in front of the Kong Family Mansion. So, we buried some of the most precious cultural relics from the Shang and Zhou dynasties in the ground. The cultural relics are irreplaceable. They are our treasures. Like our former Premier Zhou Enlai said: 'Once you ruin them, you will never know their historical value.' I agreed with this thought at the time, so I never joined the rebels.

Over the past 40 years, as China modernized and its economy thrived, it has embraced its ancient traditions with renewed pride. Nationally, Confucius has become a symbol of the extraordinary depth and continuity of Chinese civilization. In the media, his teachings are being updated for millions on national television and in schools across the land. Confucianism is back at the heart of the state curriculum.

四海孔子书院院长冯哲

FENG ZHE, Headmaster, Sihai Confucius Academy

四海孔子书院院长冯哲：

随着中国经济的腾飞，我们又开始寻找我们的精神家园的时候，孔子又开始站起来，他要在精神上站起来。所以说，一定要把孔子再请出来，甚至要活在我们心中。

这是位于北京郊区的“四海孔子书院”。3 ~ 14 岁之间的孩子们，正在用完全复古的私塾方式学习儒家经典，他们的一天从早晨五点半开始。

四海孔子书院
Sihai Confucius Academy

FENG ZHE:

With the Chinese economy thriving, we've started to seek our spiritual home, and Confucius has risen again. We need to rise spiritually. Therefore, we need to reintroduce Confucius and let him live in our hearts.

At the Sihai Academy, a Confucian boarding school on the outskirts of Beijing, children between ages 3 and 14 follow a curriculum based entirely on traditional Confucian education: Their day starts at 5:30 a.m.

四海孔子书院院长冯哲：

这个四海孔子书院的校训是诚敬、谦和。这个“诚”是做人最重要的品质，这个“谦”的意思就是，做人一定要把自己摆在一个很低的位置，才能够融合于众，最后实际上，要达到一个“和”的境界。也就是说，不仅是个人的身与心的和谐，也是人与人之间的关系的和谐。

在四海孔子书院里，孩子们不仅要接受现代的教育课程，同时还会接受孔子“六艺”课程的教育。最为重要的是，他们从很小的年龄开始，就要用心背诵并学习儒家的那些经典著作。

四海孔子书院院长冯哲：

这个自幼读中国经典，这是传统中国教育最重要的一个传统。这个小时候读经，更重要的是利用他的记忆力。因为小朋友的记忆力非常好，他不需要理解，随着年龄的增长，他的理解力逐步地增加，然后他就可以有了理解的内容。这就好比说，像那个牛起先早上把草吃进去，然后夜里再慢慢地反刍消化，第二天就转化为能量可以去工作。

或许对于当下社会来说，之所以能够让传统的儒家教育方式回归课堂，大多数人都会认为，这是由于对儒家传统伦理道德观念中“仁”这一概念的推崇。

FENG ZHE:

Our motto is sincerity, respect, humility, and harmony. Sincerity is the most important virtue of being a human being. Humility means to place yourself in a lower position and fit into the majority. The final virtue is harmony – harmony of one's body, soul, and interpersonal relationships.

At Sihai, children are instructed in the modern curriculum and the Confucian Six Arts. Crucially, they learn to recite the Confucian classics 'by heart' from a very early age.

FENG ZHE:

The purpose is to memorize because children usually have good memories; they don't necessarily have to understand. As they grow and understand more, the sentences will make more sense. This is similar to cattle eating in the morning, digesting and ruminating overnight, and gaining energy for the next day. I guess this is very different from Western education tradition.

At the core of this resurgence in Confucian education is a focus on what many feel is the most important Confucian virtue, what Confucius called '*ren*' (often translated as benevolence or humanity).

四海孔子书院吕云鹏老师：

好，下面我们来讲一讲这个字，这个字念什么，仁。我们知道儒家的教育，它是以仁爱为核心的。但是，这个“仁”是什么意思呢？想到自己就要想到别人，想到别人一定想到自己。

夏威夷大学安乐哲教授：

“仁”这个字，其实最初的意思就是人。但是，孔子用的这个字是两个人，这就是他说的，要成为一个完美的人，必须立足于我们在家庭和社会中的角色与关系，可以将每个人的角色诠释得更加完美。比如成为最好的父亲、最好的祖母、最好的老师。

回首千年之前，孔子深入求索这些思想光芒的时刻，仍然是在他到处流亡的那些岁月。奔波游走在各个诸侯国之间，虽然找不到一位明君可以采纳他的思想，但是就在孔子与弟子们的彼此对话中，他升华了“仁”的思想，继而衍生出了“恕”这一重要而被广泛传播的理念。

夫子，有一言而可以终身行之者乎。

其恕乎，己所不欲勿施于人。

TEACHER:

Now let's talk about this character, how to pronounce it? As we all know, at the core of Confucian education is benevolence. What does it mean? Whenever you think about yourself, you should think about others. Whenever you think about others, think about yourself.

ROGER AMES:

The word '*ren*' actually means person. However, Confucius uses both the character for person and the character for the number two. He is saying that the way we become consummate as human beings lies in the roles and relationships that locate us within the family and community. It should be translated as the very best conduct that one can exhibit; becoming the very best father, very best grandmother, or very best teacher.

Confucius developed this idea during his exile. Adrift within the warring states with no ruler accepting his ideas, it was during conversations with his disciples that he elaborated on the concept of *ren*, also communicating the secondary idea of empathy, what Confucius called '*shu*.'

ZIGONG: Is there one word that may serve as a rule of practice for all one's life?

CONFUCIUS: It seems to be the word 'shu.' What you do not want to be done to yourself, do not do to others. (*Analects*)

清华大学贝淡宁教授：

西方社会的一个问题，可能就是过度的个人主义。大家都在说的，什么是真我，我深入自己的内心，一旦找到答案，于是我就领悟了生命的意义。但是，儒家教导我们，你不能仅仅是深入自己的内心，你要看到你与其他人的关系。这些关系如何，如果不是出于平等心的关怀，（这些关系）就没有那么重要。最重要的就是，这些关系要以同情和关爱为特点。

如果说孔子提出的“仁”与“恕”的道德概念，是为了对抗他那个时代的个人主义，那么对很多人来说，在当今的社会仍然存在着这样的对抗。正因如此，许多中国的公司，已经开始把儒家理念纳入到现代经济活动中。

京博石化集团公司是中国最大的炼油厂之一。在这里，如同其他许多中国公司一样，“仁”和“孝”这样的儒家道德准则，早已被纳入到公司最核心的管理理念中。他们相信，这些传统价值观，不仅提升了员工的道德水平，也让公司在市场上更具有竞争力。

DANIEL BELL:

One of the problems in Western societies is arguably excessive individualism. What is the authentic self? I look deep in my heart and once I find the answer there, I can find the meaning to life. However, Confucianism says you don't just look deep in your heart, you must look at relations with other people. What are the qualities of those relations? If they're hierarchical, that's not so important. What is important is that those relations are characterized by compassion and care.

If Confucius formulated the virtues of benevolence and empathy to counter the individualism of his own time, then, to many people, this has clear parallels to the materialism of contemporary society. To this end, many Chinese companies have started to integrate Confucian ideas into the modern workplace.

One of China's largest petroleum refining factories, Chambroad Petrochemicals, in Confucius' hometown of Shandong, has made the concepts of benevolence and filial piety an essential part of their management structure. Chambroad believes these values improve the morality of every worker and make their business more competitive.

京博石化集团公司董事长马韵升
MA YUNSHENG, CEO, Chambroad Petrochemicals, Shandong Province

京博石化集团公司董事长马韵升：

为员工的父母发放敬老金，同时也发放孝工资，最后换来的是员工的努力，是付出，是为公司创造了更多的财富。那么，就是这样往复式循环的上升，是让企业更好、我们的员工更幸福。

京博石化集团公司员工马英鹏：

我叫马英鹏，在京博石化上班。在这儿上班呢，自己的家人，包括父母还有孩子，公司都能够给你照顾得很全面。关于孔子，以前了解得比较少，只是从书本上看到的一些东西。尤其是一进大门，我们的“孔子问仁”的雕像特别醒目，从来到（京博）以后，对孔子的文化了解得比较多一些了。

京博石化集团公司员工马英鹏
MA YINGPENG, Electrician, Chambroad Petrochemicals, Shandong Province

MA YUNSHENG:

We give the parents of our employees a pension, what we call a filial salary. This, in turn, encourages the employees' hard work and generates more profit for the company. This cycle of improvement makes our company stronger and the employees happier.

MA YINGPENG:

My name is Ma Yingpeng. I am an electrician. Working here means my family, including my parents and children, are well looked after by the company. I did not know much about Confucius, only a little from textbooks. Every time I come to work, the statue of Confucius by the gates attracts me. Now, I know more about him.

这样的一种商业与道德的结合，被一些学者称为“实用儒家”，可以看作儒家与时俱进的例子，现在也已经被许多人视为最具中国特点的核心竞争力。

悉尼大学王安国教授：

在我看来，儒家的价值取向在与其他国家的竞争中给了中国一些优势。比如，在经济发展中，儒家强调合作、共赢、教育、规则、学习，所有这些在当今世界都无比重要。

这是一个震撼人心的故事，尽管孔子在他的时代并不被接纳，但孔子的思想却塑造了中国人生命中最深远、最具人性光辉的部分。从孔子所在的那个礼坏乐崩的时代，穿越古老中国的千年沧桑，到21世纪重新崛起于世界的经济强国，他的思想不仅在不断延续，更是从代代相传中找到了全新的意义所在。为什么会产生如此强大的精神力量，或许是因为在他们内心深处，始终供奉着历经时间锤炼的信念，帮助他们在中国人的生命体验中找到最重要的终极意义——家。

This combination of business and virtue, what some scholars have called 'practical Confucianism,' is one example of how it has consistently evolved with the times: Some see this as giving China its competitive edge.

JEFFREY RIEGEL:

The values of Confucianism can be seen as something that gives China an advantage in its dealings with other countries, in its economic development. Confucianism emphasizes cooperation, collaboration, education, discipline, and study. All these things are important for success in the modern world.

It's a remarkable story. Rejected in his own lifetime, the teachings of Confucius have come to define the deepest and most human aspects of Chinese life. From the disorder of his own times through the legacies of China's imperial age and 21st century China's new-found status as an economic superpower, the teachings of Confucius have persisted and found new meaning with each new generation. Why have these teachings survived and thrived? At their core lies a shared set of beliefs and rituals that have withstood the test of time, finding their ultimate meaning in the most important unit of Chinese life – the family.

四川大学谢幼田教授：

中国这个制度，20 世纪以来做了很多尝试。最后中国人他的内心还是以家庭为重，因为家庭才是他的一种价值观，他的人生的着落点，他在家庭里生活，他的人生才有意义。

人们对家庭观念的尊重，可以从中国文化中最重要的一种仪式里窥见一斑：清明祭祖。儒家思想中的礼、孝、仁，一并展现其中。

孔子 72 代后裔孔宪铎
KONG XIANDUO, a 72nd generation descendant of Confucius

孔子 72 代后裔孔宪铎：

清明，一般清明不在农历的三月，或者就在二月，清明时墓上发出了青草青芽，树也发芽了。

PROF. XIE YOUTIAN:

Since the 20th century, China has experimented with many social systems. In the end, the Chinese still have family in their heart because the family is their value, their resting place in life. Only when they live in the family does life makes sense to them.

This reverence for the family is at the core of the grave-sweeping festival of Qingming, one of the most important rituals in Chinese culture, where the Confucian virtues of rite, filial piety, and benevolence converge.

KONG XIANDUO:

Tomb-sweeping Day is in spring, when everything restarts. It occurs in February or March on the lunar calendar. The grass on the tomb is green and the trees have new buds.

清明时节，一家老少来到墓前祭拜他们离世的先人，对于曲阜的这一支四世同堂的孔氏后裔来说，意味着他们要再次造访孔林这个安葬孔氏先祖的地方。

孔子 72 代后裔孔宪铎：

像我们这一片已经埋了 30 多口人了，都长眠在这里了，现在我是第 72 代。男的，偷盗（者）再就是地痞、流氓不能入祖坟，女的不孝敬公婆（者）、娼，嫖娼卖淫这个意思，她不能入祖坟，这是孔家的规矩。

孔子 74 代后裔孔繁飚
KONG FANBIAO, a 74th generation descendant of Confucius

孔子 74 代后裔孔繁飚：

有这么大一片家族墓，可能若干年以后，我也许会躺在这里，跟我的那些祖先，然后太爷爷、爷爷，然后一起长眠于此。

On Qingming, the young and old visit the graves of their parents and ancestors, which, for descendants of Confucius in Qufu, means a trip to the Cemetery of Confucius, where their family members are buried.

KONG XIANDUO:

We have more than 30 family members buried here. I'm the 72nd generation. Robbers, thieves, and rogues cannot be buried here. Neither can women who are not filial to their parents-in-law. You know what prostitutes are, right? Those women can't be buried here. This is the rule.

KONG FANBIAO:

We have such a big family cemetery. Perhaps in the future, I'll sleep here with my grandfathers and great-grandfathers forever.

孔子 72 代后裔孔宪铎：

一起磕个头，老爷爷不喝酒，先磕个头吧，来吧，磕个头，我可是跪不下了。

在曲阜，清明节成了一个孔氏众多家族成员交流聚首的良机，2015 年是孔子诞辰 2566 年。

2015 年清明孔氏后裔曲阜家祭合影

A group photo of the Kong family's sacrifice on the 2,566th anniversary of the birth of Confucius

KONG XIANDUO:

Are we all here? Now, let's do it. Grandpa doesn't drink wine, only tea. Let's kowtow together. I can hardly kneel.

In Qufu, Qingming is also an occasion when large numbers of the extended Kong family come together. 2015 marked the 2,566th anniversary of the birth of Confucius.

孔子76代后裔孔令珊：

震惊哪！就是2566年以后，孔子在历史上的作用，从今天的隆重聚会就可以表达出来，孔子在世界和中国人民心目中的重要地位和英雄形象。

孔子77代后裔孔德铭：

现在所挖掘的每个人的优点，其实就是我们孔子所提倡的优点。应该说，我也感觉很敬佩，也很荣耀，就是自己能够从事这个家族的工作。

在清明这个中国人的重要节日里，孔氏家族的后裔们纷纷前来，而他们最重要的一项仪式，就是一同追思他们最伟大而显赫的先祖——孔子。在孔子的陵墓前集体祭拜，这样的仪式在同样的地点已经举办了2000多年，而这个仪式也赋予了孔子非同寻常的文化意义。

KONG LINGSHAN:

What amazes me is that, even after 2,566 years, Confucius still holds such an important status and image in the mind of Chinese people and people worldwide.

KONG DEMING:

The virtues each person tries to live up to today are exactly those advocated by Confucius. I feel very respectful and honored to be involved in the efforts of my clan.

The gathering of the Kong family at the Qingming Festival culminates in a ceremony to worship their most important ancestor, Confucius. Conducted at the same spot for over 2,000 years, this has become a ritual of national importance given the contribution Confucius made to the Chinese and so many around the world.

孔子 76 代后裔孔令涛
KONG LINGTAO, a 76th generation descendant of Confucius

孔子 76 代后裔孔令涛：

孔子在他成长的历史时期呢，他的理想也是能恢复一个礼乐文化的鼎盛时代，用以礼治国去把社会的公民的这种伦理道德水准，以及社会的发展，上升到一个鼎盛时代。那么，作为孔子的后人，我们应该担负起一个传承和发扬的责任和使命。

孔子逝世后，他的传世思想变成了一份史无前例的文化遗产。在关于孔子的传记中，司马迁写道：公元前 478 年，在人生的最后时刻，72 岁的孔子预见到了自己即将死亡的征兆。

仲尼视之，曰：麟也，取之。曰：河不出图，洛不出书，吾已矣夫。

KONG LINGTAO:

Confucius tried to revive the culture of rituals and music and use the governance of the country with rite to improve the moral ethics of its citizens. As subsequent generations of Confucius, we need to shoulder this responsibility, to inherit it and carry it forward.

It's a remarkable legacy given the circumstances of Confucius' death. In the final chapter of the biography, Sima Qian writes that Confucius, 72 years old and despondent over his failure to have changed the world, witnessed the revisit of the *qilin*, a portent of his own death.

SIMA QIAN: Confucius saw it and said: 'It is my time. I'm going to die.'

曾经作为祥瑞的象征、预示了孔子诞生的麒麟，这一次却没有能够阻止死亡的降临。几天之后，当忠诚的弟子子贡前来探望的时候，据说孔子在此说出了他的临终遗言，那是一段来自《诗经》中的句子。

太山坏乎，梁柱摧乎，哲人萎乎。

西汉史学家司马迁：天下君王至于贤人众矣，当时则荣没则已焉，孔子布衣传十余世，学者宗之，可谓至圣矣。

Where once the *qilin* had gloriously heralded his birth, it now heralded his death. A few days later, visited by his faithful disciple Zigong, Confucius uttered his last words, a quotation from the *Book of Songs*.

The great mountain must crumble, the strong beam must break, and the wise man withers away like a plant.

SIMA QIAN: The world has known innumerable princes and worthies who enjoyed fame and honor in their day, but were forgotten after death. However, Confucius, a commoner, has been revered by scholars for over 10 generations: He is called the Supreme Sage!

附录一：摄制组名单

总 策 划	聂辰席	孙守刚	
总 监 制	李 挺	王世农	梁国典
监　　制	阚兆江	马润生	
策　　划	张广义	张林林	张　琳
	丁绍敏	蓝　海	
学术顾问	干春松	舒大刚	鲍鹏山
	孔祥林	谢幼田	杜维明
	艾　恺	安乐哲	黎瑞智
	田辰山	贝淡宁	王安国
	金安平	戴梅可	王子今
	田　青	毛佩琦	蔡德贵
	郭　沂	蒋英炬	孔德平
总 导 演	闫　东		
总制片人	闫　东		
制 片 人	张　啸	刘　玮	聂丛丛
	孙　琳		

Appendix I: Crew List

Chief Planners

Nie Chenxi / Sun Shougang

Chief Supervisors

Li Ting / Wang Shinong / Liang Guodian

Supervisors

Kan Zhaojiang / Ma Runsheng

Planners

Zhang Guangyi / Zhang Linlin / Zhang Lin
Ding Shaomin / Lan Hai

Academic Advisors

Gan Chunsong / Shu Dagang / Bao Pengshan
Kong Xianglin / Xie Youtian / Du Weiming
Guy Salvatore Alitto / Roger T. Ames / Li Ruizhi
Tian Chenshan / Daniel A. Bell / Jeffrey Riegel
Annping Chin / Micheal Nylan / Wang Zijin
Tian Qing / Mao Peiqi / Cai Degui
Guo Yi / Jiang Yingju / Kong Deping

Chief Director

Yan Dong

Chief Producer

Yan Dong

Producers

Zhang Xiao / Liu Wei / Nie Congcong
Sun Lin

执行制片人	王　露		
编 导 组	王柯庆	秦　雪	周　珏
	陈　东	孙培强	
前期采访	李　果	訾　瀚	吉　冈
文学统筹	张受庸	西　冰	
摄 影 组	金延泽	孙培强	张世君
	赵永华	袁　超	刘一鸣
	王玉国		
摄影助理	李　杨	张世恒	姚　弛
技　　术	孙　涛	孙　硕	薛思雪
	杨　辰	李鑫超	苗　晨
音乐编辑	毛薇薇		
解　　说	李立宏		
录　　音	赵　硕	康韦斯	姜　阅
	刘恒伟		
灯 光 师	吕世光		
灯光助理	米育军	崔立伟	
资料总监	倪代光		

Executive Producer

Wang Lu

Editing

Wang Keqing / Qin Xue / Zhou Yu
Chen Dong / Sun Peiqiang

Interviewers

Li Guo / Zi Han / Ji Gang

Literary Coordinators

Zhang Shouyong / Xi Bing

Videography

Jin Yanze / Sun Peiqiang / Zhang Shijun
Zhao Yonghua / Yuan Chao / Liu Yiming
Wang Yuguo

Camera Assistants

Li Yang / Zhang Shiheng / Yao Chi

Technology

Sun Tao / Sun Shuo / Xue Sixue
Yang Chen / Li Xinchao / Miao Chen

Music Editing

Mao Weiwei

Narrator

Li Lihong

Recording

Zhao Shuo / Kang Weisi / Jiang Yue
Liu Hengwei

Lighting

Lv Shiguang

Lighting Assistants

Mi Yujun / Cui Liwei

Data Director

Ni Daiguang

资　　料	张　洁	郭建芬	赵鹿影
责　　编	吴胜利	王文赫	
国际统筹	孔令涛	花　凯	李庆庆
	申家宁		
国际协调	张晓键	尹　凡	孙文静
	郭　晶	张　昕	钱希茜
	周　睿	董婧唯	游　冰
	孟　晨	习　超	阳　霏
制片主任	王建彤	刘仕平	赵晓峰
制　　片	李传海	刘　洋	孙熙雨
	尹海啸		
技术总监	栗小斌	刘　畅	关朝阳
技术协调	刘　茹	王　珮	刘　新
翻　　译	王　露	秦　雪	万　璐
	王婉莹	朱　达	
市场营销	熊　殷	谢鹏飞	王　欣
	任海平		
宣传策划	陈　忠	苑文刚	吕振亚
	刘　斌		

Data Staff

Zhang Jie / Guo Jianfen / Zhao Luying

Executive Editors

Wu Shengli / Wang Wenhe

International Coordinators

Kong Lingtao / Hua Kai / Li Qingqing
Shen Jianing

International Communicators

Zhang Xiaojian / Yin Fan / Sun Wenjing
Guo Jing / Zhang Xin / Qian Xiqian
Zhou Rui / Dong Jingwei / You Bing
Meng Chen / Xi Chao / Yang Fei

Production Management

Wang Jiantong / Liu Shiping / Zhao Xiaofeng

Production Staff

Li Chuanhai / Liu Yang / Sun Yiyu
Yin Haixiao

Technical Directors

Li Xiaobin / Liu Chang / Guan Chaoyang

Technical Coordinators

Liu Ru / Wang Pei / Liu Xin

Translators

Wang Lu / Qin Xue / Wan Lu
Wang Wanying / Zhu Da

Marketing

Xiong Yin / Xie Pengfei / Wang Xin
Ren Haiping

Publicity Planners

Chen Zhong / Yuan Wengang / Lv Zhenya
Liu Bin

宣传统筹	韩晓伦	赵津京	赵军胜
	王　莹	王立欢	刘　铭
	洪丽娟	王玉平	张延利
宣　　传	李　冰	司　楠	王　鑫
	刘　超	裴　宁	万汶柳
	刘雨涵	朱宏晨	张　强
	张曦健	李　斐	

英国摄制组

总监制	Richard Bradley
监　　制	Bill Locke
制片人	Daisy Newton Dunn
导　　演	Hugo Macgregor
摄像师	Brendan Easton
	Adam Vardy
编　　辑	Stuart Davidson
	Gabriel Edvy
	John Moffat
图式设计	Tomorrow Is Closed
原声音乐	Douglas Black Heaton

Publicity Coordinators

Han Xiaolun / Zhao Jinjing / Zhao Junsheng
Wang Ying / Wang Lihuan / Liu Ming
Hong Lijuan / Wang Yuping / Zhang Yanli

Publicity Staff

Li Bing / Si Nan / Wang Xin
Liu Chao / Pei Ning / Wan Wenliu
Liu Yuhan / Zhu Hongchen / Zhang Qiang
Zhang Xijian / Li Fei

UK Team

Chief Supervisor

Richard Bradley

Supervisor

Bill Locke

Producer

Daisy Newton Dunn

Director

Hugo Macgregor

Cameramen

Brendan Easton
Adam Vardy

Editors

Stuart Davidson
Gabriel Edvy
John Moffat

Schema Designer

Tomorrow Is Closed

Original Soundtrack

Douglas Black Heaton

录 音 师	Tloud Wang		
	Qiao Xin		
	Wu Yanbo		
	Tom Jessup		
	Dave Scaringe		

情景再现摄制组

再现指导	金铁木		
再现导演	邓 斐		
演 员	乔鸣麟	（饰 孔 子）	
	于永霖	（饰 司马迁）	
	周 东	韩永宽	蔡 华
	杨 杰	宋兴南	王博杰
制片主任	金 城		
统 筹	严 严		
摄 影	丁 哲	商 磊	
美 术	陆 斌		
灯 光	钟 城		
置 景	二 毛		
道 具	黄殿飞	韩瑞平	

Recording

Tloud Wang

Qiao Xin

Wu Yanbo

Tom Jessup

Dave Scaringe

Scene Reproduction Group

Instructor

Jin Tiemu

Director

Deng Fei

Actors Qiao Minglin (as Confucius)

Yu Yonglin (as Sima Qian)

Zhou Dong / Han Yongkuan / Cai Hua

Yang Jie / Song Xingnan / Wang Bojie

Production Manager

Jin Cheng

Coordinator

Yan Yan

Cameramen

Ding Zhe / Shang Lei

Art Design

Lu Bin

Lighting

Zhong Cheng

Gripman

Er Mao

Propsmen

Huang Dianfei / Han Ruiping

化　　妆	李　娟	朱睿娟
服　　装	张　华	杨继超
剧务主任	胡恩宇	
现场制片	蔡风东	

鸣谢单位

国家文物局

中国国家博物馆

中国艺术研究院

中国孔子基金会

北京市文物局

孔庙和国子监博物馆

山东省文物局

山东博物馆

山东石刻艺术博物馆

济宁市文物局

曲阜市文物局

曲阜电视台

荆州市委宣传部

荆州市文物保护中心

荆门市委宣传部

荆门博物馆

Makeup

Li Juan / Zhu Ruijuan

Costume

Zhang Hua / Yang Jichao

Stage Manager

Hu Enyu

On-Site Producer

Cai Fengdong

Acknowledgements

National Cultural Relics Bureau

National Museum of China

Chinese Academy of Art

China Confucius Foundation

Beijing Municipal Bureau of Cultural Relics

Confucius Temple and the Imperial College Museum

Shandong Provincial Bureau of Cultural Relics

Shandong Museum

Shandong Stone Carving Art Museum

Jining City Cultural Relics Bureau

Qufu City Cultural Relics Bureau

Qufu TV station

Jingzhou Municipal Party Committee Propaganda Department

Jingzhou City Cultural Relics Protection Center

Jingmen Municipal Party Committee Propaganda Department

Jingmen Museum

新疆吐鲁番博物馆
贵州省文物局
青岛青苹果影业有限公司

协助拍摄

山东省政府新闻办
山东广播电视台
济宁市委市政府
曲阜市委市政府
齐鲁影业传媒有限公司

联合摄制

中央电视台科教频道
英国雄狮公司
中国国际电视总公司
山东大众报业集团

中央电视台
山东省委宣传部
2016 年 1 月

Turpan Museum of Xinjiang
Guizhou Provincial Bureau of Cultural Relics
Qingdao Green Apple Film Co., Ltd

Sponsors

Shandong Provincial Government News Office
Shandong Radio and Television
Jining Municipal Government
Qufu Municipal Government
Qilu Film Media Co., Ltd

Co-Produced by

CCTV Science and Education Channel
Lion Television of the UK
China International Television Corporation
Shandong Dazhong Newspaper Group

CCTV

Shandong Provincial Party Committee
Publicity Department

January 2016

附录二：主创人员简介

制片人、总导演 闫东

闫东是中国纪录片领军人物，他以国际视野实践和表达着中国的历史与现实，30 年来创作了 30 余部纪录片。闫东导演善于驾驭题材丰富的各种项目，完成了一系列在社会上产生广泛影响的作品，令业界和广大观众称赞。多次获得中国纪录片界的各项国家级大奖。《国脉》（3D 版）获国际卢米埃大奖，《1937 南京记忆》获国际阳光纪录片节提案大奖，《中国民居》获国际 FNS 作品银奖，《博物志》入围亚广联等奖项。

主要作品：

2017 年 《港珠澳大桥》（电视版） 2 集 ×50 分钟

《港珠澳大桥》（电影版） 85 分钟

《长征》（国际版） 2 集 ×100 分钟

Appendix II: Main Crew Members

Producer & Chief Director

YAN DONG

As a leading TV documentary producer in China, Yan Dong has produced more than 30 documentaries during the past three decades, reproducing and depicting China's history and reality from a global perspective. Being talented at masterminding large projects on a variety of subjects, Mr. Yan has won acclaim from industry peers and a broad spectrum of audiences through a series of works of wide-ranging social influence, including multiple national and international prize-winners, such as *National Museum of China: 100 Years* (3D, Lumiere Award, 2013), *Memories of Nanjing, 1937* (Sunny Side of the Doc, 2014), *Residential Housing in China* (Silver, FNS, 1994), and *Natural History* (ABU Award finalist, 2014).

Main Works:

2017

Hong Kong - Zhuhai - Macao Bridge (TV version)

2 episodes × 50 minutes

Hong Kong - Zhuhai - Macao Bridge (movie version)

85 minutes

The Long March (international version)

2 episodes × 100 minutes

2006—2017年		
	《中国记忆》	10集 ×90~240分钟
2016年	《长征》	8集 ×50分钟
2015年	《孔子》	1集 ×90分钟
	《改变世界的战争》	2集 ×50分钟
	《东方主战场》	8集 ×54分钟
2014年	《1937南京记忆》	5集 ×52分钟
	《国魂》	3集 ×30分钟
2013年	《国脉3D》	1集 ×30分钟
	《国脉》	6集 ×52分钟
2012年	《大鲁艺》	5集 ×52分钟
	《科学发展铸辉煌》	7集 ×52分钟
2011年	《旗帜》	10集 ×52分钟
2010年	《大三峡》	6集 ×30分钟
	《第一犁》	3集 ×50分钟
2009年	《古田会议》	2集 ×50分钟

2006-2017

Memories of China 10 episodes × 90-240 minutes

2016

The Long March 8 episodes × 50 minutes

2015

Confucius 1 episode × 90 minutes

The War That Has Changed the World

2 episodes × 50 minutes

The Oriental Battlefield 8 episodes × 54 minutes

2014

Memories of Nanjing, 1937

5 episodes × 52 minutes

The Soul of a Nation – Socialist Core Values

3 episodes × 30 minutes

2013

National Museum of China: 100 Years (3D version)

1 episode × 30 minutes

National Museum of China: 100 Years

6 episodes × 52 minutes

2012

Luxun Art Institute 5 episodes × 52 minutes

Scientific Outlook on Development Brings Glory

7 episodes × 52 minutes

2011

The Banner 10 episodes × 52 minutes

2010

Three Gorges 6 episodes × 30 minutes

The First Plow 3 episodes × 50 minutes

2009

Gutian Conference 2 episodes × 50 minutes

2008 年	《伟大的历程》	7 集 ×52 分钟
	《开创》	1 集 ×50 分钟
2007 年	《杨尚昆》	8 集 ×52 分钟
2004 年	《百年小平》	6 集 ×52 分钟
	《无声的革命》	4 集 ×30 分钟
2001—2003 年		
	《伟大的创造》	10 集 ×30 分钟
2002 年	《走进新时代》	10 集 ×35 分钟
2001 年	《中华文明五千年》	15 集 ×50 分钟
1999 年	《李大钊》	2 集 ×50 分钟
1998 年	《共产党宣言》	2 集 ×50 分钟
	《改革开放 20 年》	12 集 ×50 分钟
1997 年	《科教兴国》	14 集 ×25 分钟
1995 年	《牡丹》	4 集 ×20 分钟
1994 年	《中国民居趣谈》	12 集 ×25 分钟

2008

The Great Pilgrimage 7 episodes × 52 minutes

The Inauguration of CCTV 1 episode × 50 minutes

2007

Yang Shangkun 8 episodes × 52 minutes

2004

Oral Histories on Deng Xiaoping: In Memorial of His 100th Birthday Anniversary 6 episodes × 52 minutes

Quiet Revolution 4 episodes × 30 minutes

2001-2003

Great Invention 10 episodes × 30 minutes

2002

Entering into a New Era 10 episodes × 35 minutes

2001

Five Thousand Years of Chinese Civilization 15 episodes × 50 minutes

1999

Li Dazhao 2 episodes × 50 minutes

1998

The Communist Manifesto 2 episodes × 50 minutes

20 Years of Reform and Opening Up 12 episodes × 50 minutes

1997

Science and Education to Rejuvenate the Nation 14 episodes × 25 minutes

1995

Peony 4 episodes × 20 minutes

1994

Residential Housing in China 12 episodes × 25 minutes

1991 年　《推销艺术电视表演赛》

1 集 ×80 分钟

1990 年　《历史的脚印》　2 集 ×25 分钟

1989 年　《神州风采——说药》

2 集 ×5 分钟

《花鼓灯》　1 集 ×30 分钟

1989 年　《中成药》　8 集 ×5 分钟

1988 年　《科学人物》

（袁隆平、曾毅、王德民、顾诵芬等）

4 集 ×20 分钟

1987 年　《邮票上的知识竞赛》

5 集 ×50 分钟

1991

TV Performance Competition on the Art of Selling

1 episode × 80 minutes

1990

Footprints of History 2 episodes × 25 minutes

1989

Highlights of China – Chinese Medicine

2 episodes × 25 minutes

Flower Drum Lantern 1 episode × 30 minutes

1989

Chinese Patent Medicine 8 episodes × 5 minutes

1988

Scientists (Yuan Longping et al) 4 episodes × 20 minutes

1987

Knowledge from Stamp Competition

5 episodes × 50 minutes

英方导演
HUGO MACGREGOR

英国著名纪录片导演，曾因纪录电影《犹太人的故事》（*The Story of the Jews*）获英国电影学院奖提名，为BBC、ARTE等知名电视台制作多部影片，如《女性的崛起》（*The Ascent of Women*）、《遇见古罗马》（*Meet the Romans with Mary Beard*）等。

主要作品：

2013年11月－2015年1月

《女性的崛起》 4集×60分钟

2013年3月－2013年7月

《卡里古拉的故事》 1集×60分钟

2012年9月－2013年3月

《西蒙·沙玛与犹太人的故事》 1集×60分钟

2012年3月－2012年8月

《仆人：楼梯下的真实生活》 3集×60分钟

2011年6月－2012年3月

《遇见古罗马》 3集×60分钟

Director, UK Team

HUGO MACGREGOR

Hugo MacGregor is a well-known British documentary director who directed *The Story of the Jews* (British Film Academy Award nominee), *The Ascent of Women*, and *Meet the Romans with Mary Beard.*

Main Works:

November 2013 - January 2015

The Ascent of Women 4 episodes × 60 minutes

March 2013 - July 2013

Caligula with Mary Beard 1 episode × 60 minutes

September 2012 - March 2013

Simon Schama's Story of the Jews

1 episode × 60 minutes

March 2012 - August 2012

Servants: The True Story of Life Below Stairs

3 episodes × 60 minutes

June 2011 - March 2012

Meet the Romans with Mary Beard

3 episodes × 60 minutes

干春松

1965 年生，浙江绍兴人，哲学博士。北京大学哲学系教授、北京大学儒学研究院副院长、博士生导师、中央党校博士生导师、中宣部马克思主义理论研究和建设工程首席专家、中华孔子学会常务副会长。研究领域：制度儒学、儒家思想研究和近现代思想文化研究。主要著有《制度化儒家及其解体》《重回王道》《保教立国》《康有为与儒学的“新世”》等作品。

舒大刚

1959 年生，中国重庆秀山人。1994 年获吉林大学历史学博士学位，现为四川大学教授、国际儒学研究院院长兼古籍整理研究所所长，博士生导师。主要从事中华国学、中国儒学、历史文献学等研究。曾出版《中国孝经学史》、《儒学文献通论》（三卷本）、《中国儒学通案》（共 10 种，已出版 3 种 22 册）等学术著作 10 多部，发表论文 130 余篇。目前正主持中国国家“211 工程”暨“985 工程”规划项目、中国孔子基金会重大项目《儒藏》编纂（已出版“史部”274 册），任首席专家兼总主编；贵阳孔学堂重点项目“大众儒学书系”主编。

Gan Chunsong

Born in Shaoxing, Zhejiang Province in 1965, Gan Chunsong has a PhD in philosophy. He is Professor of Philosophy and a PhD student adviser at Peking University, Vice-President of the Confucianism Research Institute of Peking University, and Executive Vice-President of the Chinese Confucian Academy. His research fields include institutional Confucianism, Confucian studies, and modern and contemporary ideological and cultural studies. His main publications include *Institutionalized Confucianism and Its Disintegration*, *Return to Hegemonic Rule*, *Governance through Confucianism*, *Kang Youwei and the New World of Confucianism*, etc.

Shu Dagang

Born in Xiushan, Chongqing in 1959, Shu Dagang earned a PhD in history from Jilin University in 1994. He is currently a professor, PhD student adviser, and President of the International Academy of Confucianism at Sichuan University. His research areas include Sinology, Confucianism, and historical literature studies. He has published more than 130 academic articles and more than ten treatises, including *History of Chinese Canons on Filial Piety* and *An Overview of Confucian Literature* (in three volumes). He is currently in charge of planning for several educational projects. Mr. Shu is also Chief Expert and Editor-in-Chief of *Collection of Essays on Confucianism*, compiled by the China Confucius Foundation (274 volumes in the History category have been published).

孔祥林

1951 年生。曾任孔子博物院院长，孔子研究院副院长，兼任曲阜师范大学教授、研究生指导教师。享受国务院特殊津贴。现任世界儒学大会秘书处秘书长，兼任中国孔子基金会理事，中国孔庙保护协会名誉会长等。主要从事孔子思想、孔氏家族、孔子庙研究。承担“世界孔子庙研究”“世界书院研究”国家社科基金课题，著有《世界孔子庙研究》《孔府文化研究》等 10 多部著作，在国内外发表论文 50 多篇。曾在联合国教科文组织巴黎总部、法国、美国、保加利亚、澳大利亚、马来西亚、日本、韩国、新加坡等地做过孔子及其思想的报告。

谢幼田

1980 年进入四川社科院，先后担任编辑、助理研究员、副研究员，编辑全国第一个经学研究专栏，两次参加中国最高学术刊物《中国社会科学》的论文评选讨论会。1987 年，应邀到美国斯坦福大学做研究，先后担任胡佛研究所的学者、研究员，在普林斯顿的当代研究中心发表了三篇长文《中国文化重建》。出版专著五部，如《中国政治文化论》《联俄容共与西山会议》等。2006 年退休后，担任四川大学客座教授，讲授儒学。

Kong Xianglin

Born in 1951, Kong Xianglin is the former Director of the Confucius Museum, Deputy Director of the Confucius Research Institute, and a professor and graduate student adviser at Qufu Normal University. He is also an expert beneficiary of a special academic allowance from the State Council. Currently, he serves as Secretary-General of the World Congress of Confucianism and is a council member of the China Confucius Foundation, among other roles. Mr. Kong's research areas include Confucian thought, the Confucius family tree, and Confucian temple studies. He is in charge of several state-funded social sciences research projects, including Global Confucian Temple Studies, etc. He is the author of more than 50 essays and approximately a dozen treatises, including *Global Confucian Temple Studies* and *Research on Confucius Family Mansion Culture*. He has lectured on Confucius and Confucianism at UNESCO in France, the United States, Bulgaria, Australia, Malaysia, Japan, Korea, and Singapore.

Xie Youtian

Xie Youtian joined the Sichuan Provincial Academy of Social Sciences in 1980, where he successively served as an editor, assistant research fellow, and associate research fellow. In 1987, he attended Stanford University as a Hoover Institution Research Fellow. That same year, he published three papers on the *Reconstruction of Chinese Culture* at Princeton University. Mr. Xie is the author of five treatises, including *Political Culture in China*. He has been a Visiting Professor of Confucianism at Sichuan University since 2006.

附录三：中外专家点评纪录片《孔子》

北京大学哲学系教授，北大儒学研究院副院长 干春松

我经常会看到西方人拍的思想家的纪录片，我们很自觉地会去了解掌握西方人是怎么想的，但是中国人因为没有那么好的一个产品，要让他们阅读《论语》《五经》，这又做不到，所以（《孔子》纪录片）这样的一个方式，可以引发西方人对于中国文献，或者进一步了解中国的冲动，勾起他们热切理解中国的期待。

世界儒学大会秘书处秘书长、中国孔子研究院研究员，孔子第 75 代孙 孔祥林

纪录片《孔子》叙述与采访交替，历史文献与情景再现并用，时空转换，经纬交织，生动形象地介绍了孔子的生平、思想和后世的影响。孔子思想主要介绍了礼、君子、孝、仁等核心观念，介绍中，它不是拘泥于传统观点的直白说教，而是将重点放在当代的影响与作用。孔子不是早已随风而化的古人，而是生活在我们身边、指导着我们生活的导师，孔子思想不是古董，而是仍然

Appendix III: Experts' Comments on *Confucius*

Gan Chunsong, Professor of Philosophy and Vice-President of the Confucianism Research Institute, Peking University

I watch documentaries on Western thinkers a lot, and I proactively try to understand Western ways of thinking. The lack of a good documentary on Confucius from China and the fact that Western readers find it almost impossible to read the original classics make *Confucius* a valuable means for preliminarily understanding Confucian classics and Chinese culture as a whole before developing a strong desire to know and understand more about China.

Kong Xianglin, Secretary-General / Secretariat of the World Congress of Confucianism, Research Fellow at the China Confucius Academy, and a 75th generation descendant of Confucius

Through alternate use of narratives, interviews, historical documents, and reproduction of historical events, the documentary travels back and forth in space and time as it vividly describes the life and thought of Confucius and his influence on later generations. Instead of getting bogged down in straightforward preaching of traditional doctrines, the documentary, in introducing Confucian thought, focuses on the core concepts of ritual, gentlemen (exemplary persons), filial piety, benevolence,

活在我们心中并在规范着我们日常生活的活色生香的思想。

中国艺术研究院副研究员，孔子第 77 代孙 孔德平

现已播出的国际版《孔子》和即将开拍的六集国内版《孔子》，可能不仅是传统文化史、儒学传播史上的大事件，而且也应是孔子造像史上的重要事件。纪录片《孔子》中的孔子图像，在媒材使用、制作程式、图像样式、呈现方式、传播路径、文化蕴涵，以及制像者身份和受众范围等方面，均迥异于传统的各类孔子图像。纪录片《孔子》以新媒体手段塑造孔子形象，是孔子造像的新方式。因此，仅就艺术学而言，两个版本的纪录片，不仅应该成为影视学研究的新对象，也自然应成为孔子造像学的重要研究对象。

中国纪录片研究中心主任 何苏六

我自己的观点就是，孔子绝对不只是中国的，他应该是中国人类文明当中所探索出来的一个有生命力的、现在仍可以服务于整个世界文明的，我觉得是一个基因。所以这个种子今天用另外一种方式在进行传播，这个传播我觉得是很有生命力的。在做这样一件事情的时候，创作者就已经想到了孔子的世界化，孔子的穿越时代的能力，还有孔子的生命力。观片的效果都得到了认可。我觉得这就是最大的成功。

and their influence and effect on the world today. Confucius is not an ancient gone with the times, but is instead a ready teacher living among us with his thinking, neither outdated nor dead, being a living regulator of our daily lives.

Kong Deping, Associate Research Fellow, Chinese National Academy of Art; 77th generation descendant of Confucius

The release of the international version of the documentary *Confucius* and the forthcoming six episodes of its domestic version is not merely a major event in the history of traditional culture and popularization of Confucianism, it is a major event in the history of Confucian image-making. The image of Confucius presented in this documentary differs greatly from traditional ones in terms of media and production delivery, image style and presentation, broadcast channel, cultural implications, image-maker identity, and targeted audience. What makes this documentary stand out is the use of new media in creating the image of Confucius. From an artistic perspective, these two production versions should not just become new subjects for movie and TV research, they should also be an important research topic in Confucian image-making.

He Suliu, Director, China Documentary Research Center

Confucius absolutely does not belong to China alone. Today, he has to be a vital gene of the Chinese civilization that can still be used to cater to world civilization as a whole. This gene is spreading vigorously in new ways. During the process of dissemination, producers highlighted the cosmopolitanization, timelessness, and vitality of Confucius. The recognized effect of this documentary is sufficient proof of its success.

中国广播电影电视节目交易中心总裁 马润生

《孔子》运用了一个时空交错表现再现的方式，讲述了一个距今2500多年，而和今天又有着密不可分的时代变迁的故事。第二个特点，它采用了很朴实的叙述语言讲述了一个很博大精深的乃至又平实的哲学故事。第三，我认为这部片子运用了寓言般的手法。然而，片子的开头是从一个梦中的麒麟开始的。当我们就要离开这个剧场的时候，那个麒麟的动画，我相信在你的心中，一定留下了极其深刻的印象。

中国新闻社原副社长 陈光忠

这部纪录片看完之后，好像没看够，还想继续看。一部纪录片能有这样吸引眼球乃至直达心灵的效应很不容易，它能做到这一点，我觉得就是做到了几个自觉：一个是文化的自觉，一个是审美的自觉，一个历史的自觉，一种是把握光影艺术怎么表达主题的一种自信。所以它能做得如此成功也是不容易的，真是不容易。

中央电视台原副台长 高峰

纪录片里最难拍的是思想家，在思想家里面，最难拍的是2000多年前的思想家。所以我想这个可能是拍纪录片里最难的一个主题了，而且孔子是一个每个人都有不同认识的思想家。《孔子》这部片子非常有意义，我祝贺闫东，祝贺这部片子成功。我希望将来我们有更多的反映孔子、反映孔子思想的纪录片诞生。

Ma Runsheng, President, China Radio, Film, and Television Programs Exchange Center

Confucius is about changes over time through the telling, in simple terms, of a profound, but practical, philosophical story occurring 2,500 years ago, but remaining inseparable from today's world. The documentary begins with the image of an imaginary *qilin*, a unicorn-like creature destined to impress the audience in a deep, allegorical way.

Guangzhong, former Vice-President, China News Agency

This documentary is worth watching, repeatedly. It's a feast for the eyes and mind. As a work of visual art, it demonstrates a confidence that is palpable from cultural, aesthetic, and historical perspectives. It's a huge success indeed!

Gao Feng, former Vice-President, CCTV

It's hard to produce documentaries about thinkers, especially a thinker who lived more than 2,000 years ago. Confucius is probably the most difficult thinker to feature in a documentary as everyone has a different picture of Confucius in mind. I congratulate Yan Dong for his success!

中国中央电视台外语频道节目部英籍顾问 郝明凯

儒学的基本观念被展现得很有趣味性，很好地表达出来了，在节目中专家解释得很清楚。我尤其感兴趣的是最后一部分，他们解释了儒学如何仍与现代社会相关联。工作的地方、公司试着遵守儒学的准则，尤其是给员工的父母发放养老金，这一部分很有吸引力。儒学和现代社会的关系，非常有趣。

广州市文化广播电视新闻出版局局长 陆志强

我看完了以后只是一句话，它的效果超出了我原来的预期。看完了，我的思绪从 2500 多年前回到现实的时候，我才发现，我自己的词汇很贫乏，而且语言是多么的苍白，所以无法去评价。最后我只是说，作为广州纪录片节的组织者，选择这部影片作为首映礼的观赏片，我觉得是正确的。

中国广电研发委员会副理事长、国家广电总局节目监看中心评审 王甫

这部纪录片摆脱了对孔子形象塑造及其思想阐释刻板单一的窠臼，运用国际化的视角、平民化的叙事以及现代化的价值标准，对儒家思想与当下社会思潮的联结进行了深入全面的解读，阐释了儒家思想对于解决现代社会思想难题与症结方面的重要意义，在观众当中起到了春风化雨，润物细无声的作用。

Michael Harrold, British Adviser, CCTV Foreign Language Channel

The basic principles of Confucianism were very interesting, well conveyed, and clearly and succinctly explained by the experts participating in this documentary. I was particularly interested near the end when these experts explained how Confucianism is still relevant to the modern consuming society, one example being that workplaces and companies attempt to observe the Confucian principles through pensions for parents of employees. It is fascinating how they brought Confucianism into the modern world.

Lu Zhiqiang, Director, Guangzhou Culture, Radio, Television, Press, and Publication Bureau

After traveling 2,500 years back in time with this documentary, I am so tongue-tied that I fail to find the exact words to express my feelings. All I can say is, as the host organizer, I did the right thing selecting this documentary for the grand opening of the Guangzhou Documentary Festival.

Wang Fu, Deputy Director, China Radio and Television Research and Development Committee; Program Evaluator, Television Program Monitoring Center, State Administration of Radio, Film, and Television

This documentary has freed itself from the stereotypes of Confucian image-building and ideology illustration. From a global perspective, using plain, simple narratives and modernized value standards, the documentary comprehensively interprets the link between Confucian ideology and ideological trends in society today. Confucius has elucidated the significance of Confucianism in solving ideological problems in modern society and has an edifying and spiritually nourishing effect on the general audience.

地球社区网（美国）L3C公司国际总监 谭思婷

这部纪录片让我印象深刻。看了这个版本的纪录片《孔子》，我觉得中国的声音变得可以理解。我最喜欢的部分就是普通人谈起他们为什么需要回家，他们为什么要照顾母亲。你知道当今世界的节奏非常快，总是在赶，人们的敏感性下降，有片中这样的例子非常好，我认为人们看后会进行反思。

德国杜伊斯堡－埃森大学汉学教授 托马斯·胡贝尔博士

孔子是全世界最重要的思想家之一。他的思想持久地影响着对东亚以及东南亚部分地区人们观念的形成及发展。一般而言，欧洲人对孔子和儒家思想知之甚少。因此，拍摄一部相关题材的电影就变得极其必要。《孔子》这部影片的诞生就满足了这一需求，它是一部制作专业而精良的作品。影片从历史角度描述了孔子的一生和他的贡献。

德国杜塞尔多夫孔子学院德方院长 培高德

该纪录片非常成功地融合了历史与现实——前者通过图片还原历史场景；后者则包括专家采访和一些关于现代中国的镜头。那些古装场景惟妙惟肖，十分真实可信。尤其让我印象深刻的是经典图片的动画效果，它们让静态的历史变得活灵活现。片子的剪辑也很到位，影片紧凑但又并非过于急躁，具有娱乐效果——它的开头

Stephanie Tansey, International Director, Earth Charter Communities Network, L3C

I'm really impressed with this version of *Confucius* because I feel the voice of China has become more understandable. The part I like most is that the common people talk about why they need to go home and care for their mothers. Today's world is rushed. It's really wonderful to have examples like this. I think people will watch it and be reflective.

Dr. Thomas Heberer, Professor of Sinology, University of Duisburg-Essen, Germany

Confucius is one of the world's most important thinkers. His teachings have had, and continue to have, a lasting influence on the formation and development of ideas of people in East Asia and Southeast Asia. In general, Europeans know very little about Confucius and Confucianism. That is why it is very necessary to have this professional and sophisticated piece of work that documents the life and achievements of Confucius from a historical perspective.

Cord Eberspaecher, German Director, Confucius Institute of Dusseldorf, Germany

The documentary successfully blends history and reality; history by way of pictures, reality by way of experts' interviews and scenes of contemporary China. The scenes of people wearing ancient costumes look very lifelike, authentic, and credible. What struck me was the animation of classic pictures, which gave life to static history. The editing produced a steady, unhurried rhythm that made the documentary very entertaining. The opening was captivating and effectively grabbed the viewer's attention. The

很吸引人，能一下子抓住观众的眼球。尤其是前半部分，要比孔子的故事片部分有趣。

法国巴黎周易中心主任、汉学家 夏汉生

儒家思想不仅在当代中国仍具有生命力，在当代法国亦然。孔子的很多提法，例如“己所不欲，勿施于人”“君子求诸己”“过而不改，是为过也”等都为世界文明做出了贡献。孔子的某些思想也与西方文明不谋而合，比如说他重视学习，主张通过学习不断提升自己。孔子还强调教化，不仅是中国人的万世师表，也堪称全人类的老师。此外，片中反映出的孔子治国理念、财富观念等也令人印象深刻，对西方社会同样具有借鉴意义。

法国中国电影节技术与选片顾问 龙爱乐

这是一部制作精良，贴近时代的纪录片，吸引我一气看完。该片在讲述历史和注重文化的同时又反映当代中国的面貌，因此具有十分积极的意义。该片内容生动有趣，即使对中国不甚了解的观众也会饶有兴味地观赏。与其他介质相比，电视节目的受众更广泛。

first half was more interesting than the story section.

Cyrille Javary, Sinologist and Director, Paris Zhouyi Research Center, France

Confucianism is not only very much alive in contemporary China, but also in contemporary France. Many Confucian thoughts, such as '[D]o unto others what you would have them do unto you,' '[T]he exemplary man examines himself,' and '[R]efusing to admit faults is a great fault,' have added to the world's collective wisdom. Some Confucian thoughts coincide with those of Western thinkers. For example, his emphasis on learning or education and his advocacy for self-advancement through learning are the makings of a great teacher, not just for generations of Chinese, but for humanity. In addition, Confucian concepts of state governance and his views on wealth, as reflected in the documentary, have impressive referential value for Western society.

Nol Garino, Technology and Film Selection Consultant, Chinese Film Festival in France

This is a fine documentary produced with the palpitations of the times in mind. It was so appealing, I could not help watching all of it in one sitting. It has a very positive impact because it features contemporary China while narrating China's ancient history and culture. The rich content, delivered through the popular medium of television, is of interest, even to those who know little about China.

澳大利亚野熊公司总裁 麦克·狄尔

孔子在西方是一个知名人物。我认为向他们普及孔子的故事十分重要，所以这部影片格外关键，这对于帮助西方观众理解中国观点与视角也很重要。此外，片中西方学者的观点、那些普通人的故事、精彩的历史再现，组合成一部十分成功的影片。

日本广播协会中国总局制片兼导演 黑柳诚司

比如说春节期间返乡中国人的心情，还有孔子的子孙们继承了他的思想生活在现代，这不仅仅是在中国，在美国等世界各地都得以传承，这不仅仅是 DNA 的延续，更是思想的延续，这些都在纪录片中有强烈的表达。

韩国 KBS 制片人 朴晋范

这部片子里面，讲述方式就是保持客观和公正。这个片子是跟英国合拍的，所以我很期待这个节目。不仅是亚洲国家，应该有很广泛的反响，（也可以）影响到整个世界！

Michael Tear, CEO, Wildbear Entertainment, Australia

Confucius is a well-known figure in the West. I think it is very important to spread the story of Confucius to help Westerners understand China's views and perspectives. The views of Western scholars, stories of common people, and reemergence of history are the core of this successful film.

Kuroyanagi Seiji, Producer and Director, Chinese Bureau, Japan Broadcasting Corporation (NHK)

The documentary conveys that China is not the only heir to Confucian thought: Other countries, like the United States, have also inherited it. Strong feelings about going home, and emphasis on family time during Chinese New Year, are not only in the DNA of the descendants of Confucius living today, but also deep within the soul of all Chinese around the world.

Park Jin-bum, Producer, Korean Broadcasting System (KBS)

I like the fair and objective narration. I think the documentary will enjoy broad influence in Asia and throughout the world.

附录四：学者评论

纪录片《孔子》国际版：向世界解读中华文化

毛佩琦，中国人民大学历史系教授、博士生导师

中华文化是什么，中华文化将会给世界带来什么？大型纪录片《孔子》的播出，向世界深入解读了中国文化的内涵。孔子是中国文化的重要代表，特别是在汉代以后，儒学成为中华文化主流的核心。该片以孔子的故事为切入点，无疑具有统领全局的意义。然而，孔子的故事也不是那么好讲的。第一，在经过沧海桑田般的变迁，特别是历尽劫难、浴火重生之后，我们对孔子如何认识？我们自己先要弄明白。第二，面对中国以外的人群，怎样把我们的语言变成一种国际语言？

Appendix IV: Scholars' Comments

Confucius (International Version) : Introducing Chinese Culture to the World

Mao Peiqi, Professor and PhD Student Supervisor, History Department, Renmin University of China

What is Chinese culture? What will it do to the world we live in? Since Confucius is a major representative of Chinese culture and his ideas, known as Confucianism, have become the core of mainstream Chinese culture since the Han Dynasty, the documentary *Confucius* can be seen as an in-depth interpretation of the essence of Chinese culture. The documentary begins with the overarching story of Confucius, which is not always easy to tell. For example, we need to find out, first and foremost, how we should see Confucius after having been through so many hardships and vicissitudes. Second, how do we make ourselves understood as we communicate with people outside China? Third, what is the best, most effective way to present the materials to a large television audience?

第三，面对广大电视观众，怎样使我们的叙述为人们喜闻乐见？

解决讲述难题的办法之一，就是到民间去，到现实中去，让生活在传承不息的儒学氛围里的中华大地上的人，用他们的具体活动，来诠释活着的儒学。团团围坐的家庭聚餐、虔诚的祖先祭礼、震撼人心的春节大返乡……通过观看中国人自在自为的日常生活，外国人直观地理解儒家真谛。清华大学教授贝淡宁解释说，礼存在于中国人的生活当中，通过礼，人们产生了集体归属感与被关怀感。夏威夷大学教授安乐哲说，礼表明人们对高贵的追求，对复杂、文雅、迷人、华美事物的追求。通过礼，提升了人性，摈弃了兽性。

聘请知名海内外专家，特别是外国专家，对孔子和儒学进行解读，是本片的又一个特点和优点。不少海外汉学家从自身历史文化背景出发，可能体会出中国人习而不察的东西。比如，安乐哲解释“仁”时说道，孔子要求成为完美的人，是立足于我们在家庭和社会中的角色与关系，在其中可以将每个人的角色诠释得更加完美，成为最好的父亲、最好的祖母、最好的老师等。孔子说“君子喻于义，小人喻于利”，那么“君子”如何翻译？可以译为“高贵的人”或“绅士”。贝淡宁说，更好的方法，是将君子译为“楷模”。他说，在社会中，“不

One answer to the questions above was to go to the people of China, who live within the heritage of Confucianism, and interpret Confucianism through their testimony or concrete activities, such as the annual Spring Festival migration, Chinese New Year's Eve family banquets, and ancestor worship practices. By watching the routines of common people, a foreign audience can intuitively learn the essence of Confucianism. As Professor Daniel Bell of Tsinghua University put it, 'ritual,' or '*li*,' which is commingled in the daily lives of the Chinese people, is something that gives people a communal sense of caring and belonging. In the words of Professor Roger Ames from the University of Hawaii: "Ritual stands for people's pursuit of nobility, flexibility, urbaneness, charm, and things of a gorgeous nature. Through ritual, human beings elevate their humanity and discard their beastiality."

Another feature of this documentary is interpretation of Confucianism by experts, including foreign experts. Many foreign sinologists, based on their unique historical and cultural backgrounds, may be able to decipher something new from things we are familiar with, but have failed to examine at great length. For example, Professor Roger Ames explains the concept of '*ren*' (benevolence) as becoming the best father, best grandmother, and best teacher. In other words, '*ren*' is the summary of perfect relationships in families and society. Confucius said: "The mind of the superior man, the *junzi*, is preoccupied with righteousness; the mind of the inferior man, the *xiaoren*, is preoccupied with gain." (*The Analects*) The word '*junzi*' is commonly translated as 'noble man' or 'gentleman,' but Professor Daniel Bell of Tsinghua University thinks a better translation would be 'exemplary person' because men and women are all supposed to live as

论男女，都应该努力成为君子，而立志成为君子者，则应有仁爱之心，不仅关怀家人，还追求正义与道德，不把自己的个人利益放在首位，这种追求将持续其终生，永无止境。”安乐哲认为，“西方社会的一个社会问题，可能就是过度的个人主义”。没有西方的对比，我们也会赞赏儒学提倡的仁，但是，当它和西方“过度的个人主义”相比较的时候，就更清楚了它的内涵。

面对现实，追随时代，是本片的第三个对策。本片讲述孔子的故事，不是为了发思古之幽情，而是为了彰显儒学在当代的生命力。学者谢幼田说：“20 世纪以来，中国社会制度，做了很多尝试，最后中国人的内心还是以家庭为重。家庭才是他的一种价值观。人生着落点，在家庭里生活才有意义。”耶鲁大学金安平说，孔子的天才之处在于他找到了一个道德基础，这就是移情。他认为移情能力是区别人类和动物的要素。既然人具有移情能力，为什么不发展它呢？为什么不让它服务于家庭，服务于社会，服务于国家呢？悉尼大学教授王安国说，风俗习惯像胶水一样凝聚着社会，孝、礼、仁又强势地回到中国人的生活中来。北东野村，一个曲阜附近的村庄，每天广播《弟子规》，用孝、礼、仁来进行管理，取得了显著成效。现在中国许多公司也把儒家理念，纳入到现代经济活动中，片中讲述了京博石化集团公司

examples, or exemplary persons, according to the Confucian tradition. "Somebody who strives to be a *junzi* should try to extend the love and care beyond the family: Such a person should also care about justice and morality, not just about their own self-interests. That's a lifelong struggle, one that never ends," Bell said. Bell went further to say: "One of the problems in Western societies is arguably excessive individualism." The Confucian concept of 'benevolence' is a sharp contrast to that.

The third approach of the documentary is to face reality and keep up with the times. The purpose of telling the story of Confucius is not to savor the glory of the past or lament the vicissitudes of history, but rather to reinvigorate Confucianism in the world today. As scholar Xie Youtian said: "Since the 20th century, China has tried many social systems. In the end, it's the family that counts. The family is where the average Chinese person finds the meaning of life and a sense of worth and belonging." Professor Annping Chin of Yale University says that the brilliance of Confucius lies in the fact that he was the discoverer of a moral foundation called empathy, which is a key factor separating humans from animals. "If empathy is something we are born with, why don't we expand or develop it so that it may serve the family, the community, and the state?" Professor Jeffrey Riegel, of the University of Sydney, sees the renewal of traditional Chinese values as filial piety, ritual, benevolence, and other Confucian principles return to Chinese life. "Confucius pointed out how very important those customs, and practices were, as they are the glue of society that keeps us together," he noted. Beidongye Village, a village near Qufu, Shandong Province, broadcasts *Standards for Being a Good Student and Child* every day. By resorting to the concepts of filial piety, ritual, and benevolence, the village saw

的故事。这是中国最大的炼油厂之一，公司提倡仁孝、道德，使商业与道德相结合，提高了自身的竞争力。这是“实用儒家”、儒家与时俱进的例子。

孔子不仅仅属于中国，还属于全世界。在国外，学术界对孔子的研究越来越深入，普通大众也越来越关注孔子，越来越认识到儒学的价值。中国人有责任讲好孔子的故事，不仅自己要好好继承和弘扬这份宝贵遗产，也要让全世界与我们一起共享。本片通过孔子的故事讲了中国的故事，把种种深奥的道理平易亲切地呈现在观众面前，很好地达到了预期效果，是一部有思想深度的电视艺术精品。在地球村日益缩小，各国面临的问题越来越一致，越来越成为一个命运共同体的时候，孔夫子的理论恰恰给予了解决世界问题的一个可供选择的途径。

remarkable progress in administration. Today, many corporate entities in China have incorporated Confucian concepts into their business operations. The documentary cites the case of Chambroad Petrochemicals Co., Ltd, one of the largest petroleum refineries in China, which has become more competitive combining business with moral ethics by advocating for benevolence, filial piety, and morality. This is a typical example of 'pragmatic Confucianism,' or how Confucianism can survive with the times.

Confucius belongs not only to China, but also to the world. As academic research on Confucianism becomes deeper in some foreign countries, the general public all over the world see more value in Confucianism and pay more attention to Confucius as a person. We Chinese have the responsibility to tell the story of Confucius in an accurate, appealing way because it's a precious legacy we are obligated to inherit, advocate for, and share with the world. By telling the story of China through the story of Confucius, this documentary is an insightful masterpiece of television art that reveals to the audience profound doctrines in a plain, simple, and effective way. As the global village becomes increasingly smaller, looking more like a community of shared destiny, the countries of the world are faced with more consistent issues. In this context, the theory of Confucius is certainly one of the alternatives available to tackle global issues.

寻找孔子的灵魂与终极意义

赵先权，中央电视台高级编辑、中央电视台发展研究中心电视传播研究部副主任

中外合拍的纪录片《孔子》于 2016 年元旦在中央电视台科教频道首播。这部具有国际范儿的长达 90 分钟的纪录片，不仅是献给亿万电视观众的精神大餐，也是思想文化领域的一件大事，值得引起人们高度关注和思考。

孔子，是一个永恒的话题。2000 多年来，褒贬不一，从汉代独尊儒术直到晚清，孔子及其儒家思想与帝制的亲密关系是传统的主流，然而正如该纪录片所描述的，20 世纪的批孔批儒浪潮，尤其是“文革”破“四旧”运动对孔子的极端否定，使得孔子的地位降到历史最低谷。中国近几十年在发展经济的同时，重新尊孔，并且再次认可其伦理道德价值。纪录片《孔子》在此历史与时代背景下，从国际视野寻找孔子的灵魂与终极意义，传播孔子与儒家思想的价值观，对于中国文化走出去，作用巨大！

该片的第一大亮点是人物采访。国际上著名的汉学

Seeking the Soul and the Ultimate Meaning of Confucius

Zhao Xianquan, PhD, Senior Editor, Deputy Director, TV Communication Research Department, Research and Development Center, CCTV

The Sino-UK documentary *Confucius* was first broadcast on CCTV's Science and Education Channel on January 1, 2016. Release of this 90-minute international effort was not only a spiritual feast to hundreds of millions of TV viewers, but also a major event in ideological and cultural spheres: An event that should grab people's attention and provide impetus for deep thinking.

Confucius is an eternal topic. For more than 2,000 years, comments about him have been mixed. From the Han Dynasty, when Confucianism was revered as the sole state doctrine, to the late Qing Dynasty, the close link between the imperial monarchy and Confucius, as well as his school of thought, had been the mainstream of Chinese tradition. However, as shown in the documentary, the anti-Confucius and anti-Confucianism campaigns during the 20th century, especially the complete denial of Confucius during the Cultural Revolution and the campaign to Destroy the Four Olds, plunged Confucius into the pit of history. During recent decades of economic development, China has started venerating Confucius again and has reaffirmed his moral and ethical value. Against this backdrop, the documentary's search for the soul and ultimate meaning of Confucius from a global perspective, along with its drive to disseminate Confucian values, will play a great role in the globalization of Chinese culture.

One high point of this documentary is the personal interviews. Through one-on-one interviews with world renowned sinologists, such as Professor Jeffrey Riegel of the University of Sydney, Professor Annping Chin of

家，比如悉尼大学教授王安国、耶鲁大学教授金安平、加州大学伯克利分校教授戴梅可、夏威夷大学教授安乐哲、清华大学教授贝淡宁，他们向世界观众解释孔子的内涵，很有说服力。同时，采用北京外国语大学田辰山博士的外语同期声，消除西方人士的语言接受障碍，可谓事半功倍。

故事化讲述，使得抽象理念具象化。这是该片的第二大亮点。不仅讲孔子的传奇故事，还通过今天的典型事例讲述孔子思想的生命力和影响力。比如，通过山东一个名叫北东野村的礼教缩影，说明《弟子规》儒家教化的作用；通过春节团聚的真实记录，阐述家庭、孝道的凝聚力与人情味；通过京博石化集团运用儒家文化管理企业，证明传统价值观对当代经济运行的效果；通过四海孔子书院的教育实践，给素质教育提供新的启迪。这些活生生的事实，告诉人们，孔子的灵魂已经深入世俗生活，绝不是空洞的说教。

提炼关键词，为观众找到理解孔子思想的钥匙，是该片的又一亮点。礼、君子、孝、仁、六艺，这些内涵丰富的汉字词汇，是儒家经典的精华。比如，君子，不仅是精英领导者的楷模，也是一般人学习的榜样。做人，就是要做具有君子人格的人，君子喻于义、小人喻于利！今天，我们看看拜金主义对道德的损害，就更加理解义

Yale University, Professor Michael Nylan of UC Berkeley, Professor Roger Ames of the University of Hawaii, and Professor Daniel Bell of Tsinghua University, the documentary provides convincing interpretations of Confucius for a global audience. In addition, Dr. Tian Chenshan, of the Beijing Foreign Studies University, spoke English instead of his mother tongue, Chinese, for the benefit of English speakers. That was a thoughtful act and kills two birds with one stone.

The second highpoint is the narrative style that puts abstract ideas into concrete stories. These stories not only include legends and biographical anecdotes of Confucius, they also include present-day showcases and examples illustrating the vitality and influence of Confucian ideology. For example, the story of Beidongye Village in Shandong Province demonstrates the enlightening and transforming role of ritual as people of that village adhere to Confucian canon entitled *Standards for Being a Good Student and Child*. Through true accounts of Chinese New Year reunions, the documentary describes family cohesion, filial piety, and human interest. Chambroad Petrochemicals Co., Ltd proves the effect of traditional values on economic operations today through their application of Confucianism in corporate management. Through the educational practices of the Sihai Confucius Academy (in Shandong Province), the documentary provides new insight for quality education. These real-life stories tell us that the soul of Confucius and the spirit of Confucianism have reached deep into people's lives.

The third highpoint is extraction of key words, which grants the audience a key into the thoughts of Confucius. Meaningful concepts, such as '*li*' (ritual), '*junzi*' (exemplary person), '*xiao*' (filial piety), '*ren*' (benevolence), and '*liuyi*' (Six Arts), are the quintessence of Confucian classics. For example, a *junzi* can serve as an example for both elites and commoners. "A *junzi* is preoccupied with righteousness, while a *xiaoren* (inferior man) is preoccupied with personal gain." In life, one should strive to be a person with the virtues

的重要性。曾经有过一种观点，认为中国传统农业社会轻视商业利益，导致社会发展迟缓。而事实证明，唯利是图也绝不是市场经济的唯一选择，普通人做人也不能见利忘义。否则，就会丧失道德底线。人们呼唤儒商，崇尚义利平衡，特别是主流价值观提倡为官、发财两分开，已经说明君子的德行毕竟是真正的正能量。纪录片《孔子》重新让儒家思想发扬光大，对于世道人心大有裨益。

此外，该片在叙事结构上采取经纬交织、时空转换的方式，避免了枯燥乏味，能够激荡人的思想。情景再现与影视资料的丰富运用，增加了可视性和感染力。精美的片花穿插，消除了观众的收视疲劳。显然，主创团队具有国际化的业务素质，体现了追求精品力作的实力。

最后再赘述一笔，窃以为，大型纪录片是传统电视媒体的核心竞争力之一。弘扬主流价值观，是央视等主流媒体的社会责任。电视观众为之叫好！

of a *junzi.* Today, we have a better idea of the importance of righteousness as we witness the negative impact on social mores resulting from money worship. Previously, there was a view that lack of emphasis on commercial interests in the traditional Chinese agrarian society had resulted in slow social development. Today, however, it has been proved that a self-centered value system is by no means the only option for market economy. The ordinary person living an ordinary life should not sacrifice righteousness for self-interest. Otherwise, we are in for a moral shipwreck. People call for Confucian merchants and appreciate a proper balance between profit and righteousness. Particularly, the mainstream value system repudiates official profiteering. Since the Confucian ideal of a virtuous *junzi* is pure positive energy, the documentary Confucius is doing immense good for the social mores and human soul by reinvigorating Confucian ideology.

Fourth, structurally, the documentary narrates through spatio-temporal transformation and the interweaving of historical and contemporary perspectives to stimulate thinking and avoid monotony and mediocrity. Diverse use of movie and video data and reproduction of real-life sights and sounds have helped increase the documentary's popular appeal. The well-designed trailers can also help the audience relax visually during the viewing process. Obviously, the production team has proved their professional caliber and global vision to create a masterpiece.

Last but not least, since full-length documentaries are a core area of competitiveness for traditional television, mainstream media outlets like CCTV have the social obligation to use them in promoting mainstream values. I am certain TV viewers will approve of such endeavors.

附录五：孔子“和而不同”的思想指导我创作纪录片《孔子》*

尊敬的各位来宾、女士们、先生们：

大家好！我代表纪录片《孔子》摄制组感谢大家参加今天的新闻发布会。

两年前，我和英国雄狮公司沟通《孔子》的细节故事，我请雄狮公司在本土做个调研，他们告诉我，见到两位英国普通人就一个疑难问题争论不休，没有答案，经常落下一句话，这么高深的问题到遥远的中国请教孔子吧！经过央视台领导李挺副总编辑的决策，我们经过深入考察，决定邀请雄狮公司和我们联合制作纪录片《孔子》，充分调动我们东西方不同思维和视角融合后呈现出全球观众喜欢看的纪录片。

---

* 本文为总导演闫东 2015 年 10 月 22 日在英国伦敦兰卡斯特宫纪录片《孔子》国际版上线新闻发布会上的现场发言。

Appendix V: Application of the Confucian Concept of 'Harmony in Diversity' in the Production of *Confucius*[*]

Distinguished Guests, Ladies and Gentlemen,

Hello! On behalf of the *Confucius* crew, I appreciate everyone comingto today's press conference!

Two years ago, while communicating with Lion Television about the details of the documentary *Confucius*, I was impressed when my partners told me they heard two British nationals jokingly talk about consulting China's Confucius over an issue they were arguing about. After in-depth investigation, with backing from Li Ting, Deputy Editor-in-Chief of CCTV, we decided to co-produce *Confucius* with Lion Television. Our plan was to produce, based on different ways of thinking from different perspectives, a documentary that would appeal to a global audience.

A year ago, on September 28, a thunderstorm struck during the live broadcast of a memorial marking the 2,565th birth anniversary of Confucius, but the rain stopped by the time we started shooting *Confucius*. I took that as Confucius blessing the

---

* This is a speech made by Yan Dong, Director of the documentary *Confucius*, on October 22, 2015, at a press conference in London's Lancaster House marking the online release of the international version of *Confucius*.

我记得一年前 2014 年 9 月 28 日，孔子诞辰 2565 年公祭大典直播，当天下着暴雨，直到《孔子》纪录片开拍仪式进行时，大雨停了下来。我在想，这分明是孔子“显圣”，预祝纪录片顺利圆满完成。美好的祝愿一直激励着中英团队，孔子《论语》中“和而不同”成为常态，多次创作灵感会议沟通没有成为负担，却成为打开我们思想的钥匙。

90 分钟的内容结构由孔子其人、传奇、哲学、至圣先师、传承、当今 6 个单元组成，近 80% 的篇幅纪录孔子思想活在当下的朴素真实的故事，20% 情景再现历史上的孔子家族众生相、孔子周游列国、孔子有教无类收徒授课、司马迁写作《孔子世家》等场景。毫无疑问，这是一项艰巨的挑战，也是一次有益的合作。经过两年多的创作历程，我和摄制组每一位成员深深感受到，孔子不仅仅是属于中国，更是属于世界的。他的许多思想和观念在世界上已产生广泛共鸣并渗透于人们今天的生活之中，我们力图塑造的纪录片中的孔子有传奇智慧有温暖人性，他一定是活在当下的孔子。

闫东

documentary. With such a blessing, the Sino-British team labored in harmony in a culturally diverse setting commensurate with the teachings of Confucius in the *Analects*. The collaborative process became a fountain of creative ideas and a key to mutual understanding rather than an occasion for culture shock.

In 90 minutes, the six-episode documentary talks about Confucius the person, Confucius the legend, Confucian philosophy, Confucius the Great Sage and Master, Confucius the Living God, and Confucius in the world today. Eighty percent of the documentary is true stories of real people living under the influence of Confucian thinking, while twenty percent is reproduction of the lives and experiences of descendants of the Confucian family, the travels of Confucius in neighboring states, his teachings and discipleship training, and Sima Qian's account of Confucius' family history. Undoubtedly, this was both a daunting challenge and a beneficial cooperative project. During the over two year production process, each crew member and I felt deeply that Confucius does not belong exclusively to China, but belongs even more to the world. Since many of his doctrines and concepts have created widespread resonance in the world and infiltrated people's lives today, Confucius has a living influence on people's lives with his legendary wisdom and warm humanism.

Yan Dong

CREATIVITY
IS
GREAT
BRITAIN

中英合拍纪录片《孔子》即将全球上线
新闻发布会
News Conference for World-Wide Premiere of
CONFUCIUS
A China-UK Jointly Made Documentary
中国中央电视台主办

AFTERWORD

后记

国之交在于民相亲，民相亲在于心相通。我们在策划、拍摄纪录片《孔子》国际版前，通过对西方市场的调研，发现西方人对孔子的认知还停留在较浅的层面。德国汉学家托马斯·海贝勒在与我们交流时曾说，欧洲人对孔子和儒家思想知之甚少，因此，拍摄一部纪录片让世人了解孔子、了解其思想、了解其思想的当代意义和价值就变得非常必要。

《孔子》国际版的摄制组是由中国和英国的创作人员共同组成的。搭建这样一个国际化团队是为了从创作源头把握纪录片的国际化表达。在创作过程中，触及纪录片的文化传统、社会价值、美学标准、历史评估等问题时，中英团队由于文化背景、信仰、价值观的不同产生过许多矛盾和分歧。但是，双方对专业精神和艺术品质的追求以及传承儒学文化和开展中西交流的目标是一致的。双方通过无数次的越洋电话、会议和对话，在不断论辩、切磋、磨合中逐步取得一致，顺利完成了拍摄制作，缔结了深厚友谊。合作过程鲜明地体现了孔子“和而不同”的思想。

90 分钟的国际版纪录片用 80% 的篇幅讲述了孔子这位思想家在普通中国人心中的重要地位以及对现代中国产生的意义。坐火车回家的务工者，在孔庙工作的年轻学者，在石化公司上班的员工……英方导演克服语言

The key to sound relations between states lies in friendship between their peoples, which largely stems from mutual understanding. Our Western market survey during the planning stage of the documentary *Confucius* showed that Westerners had a relatively shallow understanding of Confucius. German sinologist Thomas Heberer said in an interview that Europeans knew very little about Confucius and Confucian ideology. Thus, we felt a compelling need to create a documentary that would help people throughout the world gain a better understanding about Confucius, his doctrines, and their contemporary implications and value.

The international version of *Confucius* is produced by a team of Chinese and British crew members. Such an international team was meant to reach an international audience from the very start of the creative process. While working together, these crew members, of different nationalities, cultural backgrounds, faiths, and values, had various disputes and conflicts over cultural traditions, social values, aesthetic standards, and historical evaluations concerning the documentary. However, because we shared the same pursuit of professionalism and art and the common goal of carrying out bilateral cultural exchange, we came to terms and reached resolution through debate, discussion, and give and take. Consequently, apart from bringing the project to a successful conclusion, we were able to build a deep and strong friendship. The cooperation was, in itself, good testimony to the Confucian doctrine of 'harmony in diversity.'

Eighty percent of the 90-minute international version talks about the weight of Confucius the thinker in the hearts and minds of the average Chinese person and his impact on modern China. With help from interpreters, our British director spent a lot of time interviewing people from different sectors, including migrant workers traveling back home

障碍在拍摄前期花了大量时间与不同职业身份的受访人面对面交流，建立信任，以捕获最自然的情感流露。

文化是沟通世界各族人民心灵的桥梁。孔子不仅是中国的，也是世界的，我们想让全球的观众看到一部不同以往的中国历史纪录片，还原一个活生生的孔子，一个有血有肉的人。法国文艺评论家艾莲娜·罗谢特在《电视全览》杂志上撰文称，《孔子》这部纪录片致力于勾勒出这位“以德治国”理论家的坎坷人生，并着重表现这位圣人如何根据其生活的时代特征来构筑其思想体系。该片从孔子门徒的记述和司马迁写的传记出发，呈现了儒家学说的概貌，并分析了儒家理论如何在改革开放时期的中国广受推崇和复兴的原因。

在《孔子》国际版的创作中，片子可以放大哪些部分，是价值观的体现，是由导演思想决定的。所有创作始终在我的把控之中。几乎所有重要的现场我都亲自把关，不放过任何细节。可以说，我用心血在拍摄。走进孔子的过程，是痴痴情深和理性思考的过程。我这样的年纪与阅历，得做出能够留得住的片子了。

2017 年 7 月 28 日，国家新闻出版广电总局国际合作司马黎司长一行来到中央电视台科教频道，围绕“合拍纪录片如何讲好中国故事”的主题进行专题调研。她充分肯定科教频道近年来在国际合作纪录片上取得的成

by train, a young scholar working at the Temple of Confucius, and an employee working in a petrochemical company. By talking with them and building rapport and trust, he captured the most sincere moments of their emotional outflow.

Culture is a bridge that links the hearts and minds of people from different nations. Confucius belongs both to China and the world. We wanted to present our global audience with a documentary about China that differed from previous endeavors and reproduce a real, living Confucius as a man of flesh and blood. French literary critic Elaine Rochette commented in *Télérama* (a journal in France) that the documentary *Confucius* shows a commitment to portraying the tortuous life of a theoretician who advocated 'rule by virtue' and emphasizes how the Sage constructed his ideological system in response to the circumstances of his time. Based on disciple accounts of Confucius and a biography written by Sima Qian, this documentary gives an overview of Confucianism and analyzes the reason why Confucian theories have revived and prospered in China during the reform and opening up period.

As chief director of the documentary, I had the final say on what to focus on and what details to include: They definitely reflect my value system. In fact, I had control over everything on almost all important subjects and scenes. In other words, I was shooting the documentary with my heart and soul. Therefore, this was a process of deep emotional involvement and rational thinking. Given my age and experience, I knew it was time for me to produce something worth keeping.

On July 28, 2017, Ma Li, Director of the International Cooperation Department under the State Administration of Press, Publication, Radio, Film, and Television, along with other leaders, came to the Science and

绩，希望我们进一步和英国雄狮公司联合创作《老子》，深入挖掘中国的思想文化遗产，建议考虑能否形成系列选题，继续探索主旋律作品的国际表达。

虽然相隔千山万水，中国与世界心与心的沟通、情与情的交往在跨越时空的纪录片中得到汇聚。中国主旋律纪录片走向国际，既需要一个文化交流融合的过程，也需要很多时代与历史的机遇。近年来，中国不断加大与西方国家的文化交往，通过共同努力，携手并肩，使中西方的文化交流与合作向着更加深入、更加持久、更加务实的方向发展。

我们正处于纪录片创作的最好时代，《孔子》在国际电视市场的成功，让我们有了更多的文化自信和文化担当。源远流长的东方智慧，伴随着中华民族的伟大复兴日益走近世界舞台，我相信，主旋律纪录片作为承载和呈现东方智慧的文化使者，将焕发出前所未有的中国魅力。

闫东

Education Channel of CCTV (CCTV-10) to conduct a field study on "how co-produced documentaries can best tell the China story." She commended CCTV-10 for its achievements in international cooperation, especially in the area of documentary co-production. She expressed hope that we would further cooperate with Lion Television in reproducing *Laozi*, along with China's other ideological and cultural legacies, so they may constitute a global documentary series with positive, main-theme content.

Though separated by numerous geographical boundaries, China and the world can communicate spiritually and emotionally across time and space through this documentary. To have China's main-theme documentaries go global, we not only need a process of cultural exchange and integration, but also the many opportunities granted by time and history. In recent years, China has been strengthening cultural exchange with Western countries. Through concerted teamwork, we have directed Sino-Western cultural exchange and cooperation toward deeper, longer-lasting, and more practical channels.

We are in the best of times for documentary production. The success of *Confucius* in the international television market has boosted our cultural confidence and cultural sense of responsibility. Today, in tempo with the gradual rejuvenation of the Chinese nation, Eastern wisdom dating back to ancient times is moving ever closer to the world's center stage. We have reason to believe that positive, main-theme documentaries will illuminate unprecedented China glamour as cultural emissaries of Eastern wisdom.

Yan Dong

图书在版编目（CIP）数据

孔子：Confucius：汉英对照 /《孔子》摄制组著；闫东主编．-- 北京：新世界出版社，2018.1
ISBN 978-7-5104-6443-0

Ⅰ．①孔… Ⅱ．①孔… ②闫… Ⅲ．①孔丘（前 551－前 479）－传记－汉、英 Ⅳ．① B222.2

中国版本图书馆 CIP 数据核字 (2017) 第 265131 号

孔子 CONFUCIUS（汉英对照）

作　　者：《孔子》摄制组
主　　编：闫　东
责任编辑：李晨曦　李莎莎
装帧设计：贺玉婷
责任印制：王宝根　苏爱玲
出版发行：新世界出版社
社　　址：北京市西城区百万庄大街 24 号（100037）
发 行 部：（010）6899 5968　（010）6899 8705（传真）
总 编 室：（010）6899 5424　（010）6832 6679（传真）
网　　址：http://www.nwp.cn
　　　　　http://www.nwp.com.cn
版 权 部：+8610 6899 6306
版权电邮：nwpcd@sina.com
印　　刷：北京东方宝隆印刷有限公司
经　　销：新华书店
开　　本：880mm×1230mm　1/32
字　　数：145 千字　　印张：7.375
版　　次：2018 年 1 月第 1 版　2018 年 1 月第 1 次印刷
书　　号：ISBN 978-7-5104-6443-0
定　　价：68.00 元

版权所有，侵权必究
凡购本社图书，如有缺页、倒页、脱页等印装错误，可随时退换。
客服电话：（010）6899 8638